The Aquaria

SAGITTARIUS

Bernard Fitzwalter has been interested in astrology since he was about six, when he played King Herod's astrologer in his primary school nativity play. For the past six years he has been teaching astrology for the Marylebone-Paddington Institute, and for seven years he has had a regular column in OVER 21 magazine. In 1984 he appeared in the first series of Anglia Television's *Zodiac Game*, which prompted the *Daily Mirror* to say that he was 'enough to give astrology a good name'.

AQUARIAN SUN SIGN GUIDES

SAGITTARIUS

22 NOVEMBER ~ 21 DECEMBER

Bernard Fitzwalter

Cover illustration by Steinar Lund
Cover typography by Steven Lee

THE AQUARIAN PRESS
Wellingborough, Northamptonshire

First published 1987

© BERNARD FITZWALTER 1987

All rights reserved. No part of this book may be reproduced or utilized in any form or by any means, electronic or mechanical, including photocopying, recording or by any information storage and retrieval system, without permission in writing from the Publisher.

British Library Cataloguing in Publication Data

Fitzwalter, Bernard
Sagittarius.— (The Aquarian sun sign guides)
1. Zodiac
I. Title
133.5'4   BF1728. A2

ISBN 0-85030-584-5

*The Aquarian Press is part of the
Thorsons Publishing Group*

Printed and bound in Great Britain

Contents

Page

Introduction   7

PART 1: HOW THE ZODIAC WORKS

1. The Meaning of the Zodiac   11
2. The Planets and the Horseshoe   19

PART 2: YOURSELF—AND OTHERS

3. The Essential Sagittarius   25
   What it means to be a Sagittarius   25
   Early, Middle or Late? The decanates   29
   Three phases of life: Sagittarius as child, adult, parent   31
4. Sagittarius Relationships   35
   How zodiacal relationships work   35
   The Sagittarius approach to relationships   41
   Individual compatibilities sign by sign   44

PART 3: YOUR LIFE

5. The Year within Each Day   69
   What does the Ascendant do?   74
   The astrology of illness   75
   Your Ascendant   76
6. Three Crosses: Areas of Life that Affect Each Other   89
   Angular houses   90
   Succedent houses   93
   Cadent houses   97

PART 4: SAGITTARIUS TRIVIA

7. Tastes and Preferences   101
      Clothes   101
      Food and Furnishings   102
      Hobbies   103
8. Sagittarian Luck   105

   A Final Word   109

Introduction

This book has been written to help you find out a little about astrology and a lot about yourself. It explains, for the first time, the motives and aims that guide your actions and make you do things the way you do; what it does not do is give you a list of 'typical Sagittarius' things to see if you recognize any of them. You are not likely to be typical anything: you are unique. What you *do* have in common with others who have birthdays at about the same time as you is a way of using your energy, a way of thinking, a set of motives and beliefs which seem to make sense to you, and which other people, those of the other eleven signs, obviously do not have. This book shows you those motives and beliefs, and shows you how they fit in with those of the other eleven signs. The zodiac is like a jigsaw: all the pieces have to be there for the whole picture to emerge.

This book also sets out to answer some very simple questions which are often asked but seldom answered. Questions like 'Why does the zodiac have twelve signs?' and 'What does being a Sagittarius actually mean?' as well as 'Why are Sagittarians supposed to be cheerful? Why can't they be morose instead? and why don't all the people of the same star sign look the same?'

The reason that these questions are seldom answered is because all too many astrologers don't know the rudiments of astrological theory, and what they do know they don't tell, because they think it is too difficult for the man in the street to understand. This is obvious nonsense: astrology was devised for and by people who did not normally read or write as much as we do, nor did they all have PhDs or the equivalent. The man in the street is quite capable of understanding anything provided that it is shown simply and clearly, from first principles upwards, and provided he has sufficient interest. Buying this book is evidence enough of your interest, and I hope that the explanations are simple enough and clear enough for you. If they are not, it is my fault, and not that of astrology.

How to Use this Book

The book is in four parts. It is best to read them in sequence, but if you have neither time nor patience, then they each work individually. Part 2 does not assume that you have read Part 1, though it helps. Part 3 makes a lot more sense if you have already read Parts 1 and 2, but it isn't mandatory. Part 4, although just as firmly based on astrological principles as the other three, is deliberately intended as light relief to bring you back to real life gently after some of the more thought-provoking stuff.

The first part of the book deals with the theory behind the zodiac; it sets out the principles of astrology and enables you to see why Sagittarius is assigned the qualities it has, how the ruling planet system works, and what all the other signs are like in terms of motivation, so you can compare them to your own. There is a short and effective method given for assessing the aims and motives of other people. When you read Part 3 you will need to know a bit about the other signs, as you will be finding out that you have more to you than just the Sagittarius part you knew about.

The second part describes the essential Sagittarius. It shows you how there are different sorts of Sagittarians according to where your birthday falls in the month, and shows how Sagittarian energy is used differently in the Sagittarius as a child, adult, and parent.

Since you spend the greatest part of your life in dealing with other individuals, the way Sagittarius deals with relationships is treated in some detail. This is the largest section of the book.

The third part shows you a different kind of zodiac, and enables you to go into your own life in much greater detail. It isn't complicated, but you do need to think. It crosses the border between the kind of astrology you get in the magazines, and the sort of thing a real astrologer does. There's no reason why you can't do it yourself because, after all, you know yourself best.

The fourth part shows you the surface of being a Sagittarius, and how that zodiacal energy comes out in your clothes, your home, even your favourite food. The final item of this part actually explains the mechanics of being lucky, which you probably thought was impossible.

I hope that when you finish reading you will have a clearer view of yourself, and maybe like yourself a little more. Don't put the book away and forget about it; read it again in a few months' time—you will be surprised at what new thoughts about yourself it prompts you to form!

Note

Throughout this book, the pronouns 'he', 'him', and 'his' have been used to describe both male and female. Everything which applies to a male Sagittarian applies to a female Sagittarian as well. There are two reasons why I have not bothered to make the distinction: firstly, to avoid long-windedness; secondly, because astrologically there is no need. It is not possible to tell from a horoscope whether the person to whom it relates is male or female, because to astrology they are both living individuals full of potential.

BERNARD FITZWALTER

Part 1

How the Zodiac Works

1. The Meaning of the Zodiac

Two Times Two is Four; Four Times Three is Twelve

It is no accident that there are twelve signs in the zodiac, although there are a great many people who reckon themselves to be well versed in astrology who do not know the reasons why, and cannot remember ever having given thought to the principles behind the circle of twelve.

The theory is quite simple, and once you are familiar with it, it will enable you to see the motivation behind all the other signs as well as your own. What's more, you only have to learn nine words to do it. That's quite some trick—being able to understand what anybody else you will ever meet is trying to do, with nine words.

It works like this.

The zodiac is divided into twelve signs, as you know. Each of the twelve represents a stage in the life cycle of solar energy as it is embodied in the life of mankind here on our planet. There are tides in this energy; sometimes it flows one way, sometimes another, like the tides of the ocean. Sometimes it is held static, in the form of an object, and sometimes it is released when that object is broken down after a period of time. The twelve signs show all these processes, both physical and spiritual, in their interwoven pattern.

Six signs are used to show the flowing tide, so to speak, and six for the ebbing tide. Aries, Gemini, Leo, Libra, Sagittarius, and Aquarius are the 'flowing' group, and the others form the second group. You will notice at once that the signs alternate, one with the other, around the zodiac, so that the movement is maintained, and there is never a concentration of one sort of energy in one place. People whose Sun sign is in the first group tend to radiate their energies outwards from themselves. They are the ones who like to make the first move, like to be the ones to take command of a situation, like to put something of themselves into whatever they are doing. They don't feel right standing on the sidelines; they are the original have-a-go types. Energy comes out of them and is radiated towards other people, in the same way as the Sun's energy is radiated out to the rest of the solar system.

The people in the other signs are the opposite to that, as you would expect. They collect all the energy from the first group, keeping it for themselves and making sure none is wasted. They absorb things from a situation or from a personal contact, rather than contributing to it. They prefer to watch and learn rather than make the first move. They correspond to the Moon, which collects and reflects the energy of the Sun. One group puts energy out, one group takes it back in. The sum total of energy in the universe remains constant, and the two halves of the zodiac gently move to and fro with the tide of the energies.

This energy applies both to the real and concrete world of objects, as well as to the intangible world of thoughts inside our heads.

A distinction has to be made, then, between the real world and the intangible world. If this is done, we have four kinds of energy: outgoing and collecting, physical and mental. These four kinds of energy have been recognized for a long time, and were given names to describe the way they work more than two thousand years ago. These are the elements. All the energy in the cosmos can be described in the terms of these four: Fire, Earth, Air, Water.

Fire is used to describe that outgoing energy which applies to the real and physical world. There are three signs given to it: Aries, Leo, and Sagittarius. People with the Sun in any of these signs find themselves with the energy to get things going. They are at their best when making a personal contribution to a situation, and they expect to see some tangible results for their efforts. They are sensitive to the emotional content of anything, but that is not their prime concern, and so they tend to let it look after itself while they busy themselves with the actual matter in hand. Wherever you meet Fire energy in action, it will be shown as an individual whose personal warmth and enthusiasm are having a direct effect on his surroundings.

Earth is used to describe the real and physical world where the energies are being collected and stored, sometimes in the form of material or wealth. The three signs given to the element are Taurus, Virgo, and Capricorn. Where Fire energy in people makes them want to move things, Earth energy makes them want to hold things and stop them moving. The idea of touching and holding, and so that of possession, is important to these people, and you can usually see it at work in the way they behave towards their own possessions. The idea is to keep things stable, and to hold energy stored for some future time when it will be released. Earth Sun people work to ensure that wherever they are is secure and unlikely to change; if possible they would like the strength and wealth of their situation to increase, and will work towards that goal. Wherever you meet Earth energy in action, there will be more work being done than idle chat, and there will be a resistance to any kind of new idea. There will be money being made, and accumulated. The idea of putting down roots and bearing fruit may be a useful one to keep in mind when trying to understand the way this energy functions.

Air is used to describe outgoing mental energies; put more simply, this is communication. Here the ideas are formed in the mind of the individual, and put out in the hope that they can influence and meet the ideas of another individual; this is communication, in an abstract sense. Gemini, Libra, and Aquarius are all Air signs, and people with the Sun in those signs are very much concerned with communicating their energies to others. Whether anything gets done as a result of all the conversation is not actually important; if there is to be a concrete result, then that is the province of Fire or Earth energies. Here the emphasis is on shaping the concept, not the reality. There is an affinity with Fire energies, because both of them are outgoing, but other than that they do not cross over into each other's territory. Wherever you meet Air energy in action, there is a lot of talk, and new ideas are thrown up constantly, but there is no real or tangible result, no real product, and no emotional involvement; were there to be emotional content, the energies would be watery ones.

Water is the collection of mental energies. It is the response to communication or action. It absorbs and dissolves everything else, and puts nothing out. In a word, it is simply feelings. Everything emotional is watery by element, because it is a response to an outside stimulus, and is often not communicated. It is not, at least not in its pure sense, active or initiatory, and it does not bring anything into being unless transformed into energy of a different type, such as Fire. Cancer, Scorpio and Pisces are the Water signs, and natives of those signs are often moody, withdrawn, and uncommunicative. Their energy collects the energy of others, and keeps their mental responses to external events stored. They are not being sad for any particular reason; it is simply the way that energy works. It is quite obvious that they are not showing an outgoing energy, but neither have they anything tangible to show for their efforts, like the money and property which seem to accumulate around Earth people. Water people simply absorb, keep to themselves, and do not communicate. To the onlooker, this appears unexciting, but there again the onlooker is biased: Fire and Air energies only appreciate outgoing energy forms, Earth energies recognize material rather than mental energies, and other Water energies are staying private and self-contained!

We now recognize four kinds of energy. Each of these comes in three distinct phases; if one zodiac sign is chosen to represent each of these phases within an element, there would be twelve different kinds of energy, and that would define the zodiac of twelve, with each one showing a distinct and different phase of the same endless flow of energy.

The first phase, not surprisingly, is a phase of definition, where the energies take that form for the first time, and where they are at their purest; they are not modified by time or circumstance, and what they aim to do is to start things in their own terms. These four most powerful signs (one for each element, remember) are called cardinal signs: Aries, Cancer, Libra, Capricorn. When the Sun enters any of these signs, the seasons change; the first day of the Sun's journey through Aries is the first day of spring, and the Spring equinox; Libra marks the Autumnal equinox, while Cancer and Capricorn mark Midsummer's Day and the shortest day respectively.

The second phase is where the energy is mature, and spreads itself a little; it is secure in its place, and the situation is well established, so there is a sort of thickening and settling of the energy flow. Here it is at its most immobile, even Air. The idea is one of maintenance and sustenance, keeping things going and keeping them strong. This stage is represented by Taurus, Leo, Scorpio, and Aquarius, and they are called, unsurprisingly, fixed signs. These four signs, and their symbols, are often taken to represent the four winds and the four directions North, South, East and West. Their symbols (with an eagle instead of a scorpion for Scorpio) turn up all over Europe as tokens for the evangelists Luke, Mark, John and Matthew (in that order).

The final phase is one of dissolution and change, as the energy finds itself applied to various purposes, and in doing so is changed into other forms. There is an emphasis on being used for the good, but being used up nonetheless. The final four signs are Gemini, Virgo, Sagittarius, and Pisces; in each of them the energies of their element are given back out for general use and benefit from where they had been maintained in the fixed phase. It is this idea of being used and changed which leads to this phase being called mutable.

Three phases of energy, then; one to form, one to grow strong and mature, and one to be used, and to become, at the end, something else. Like the waxing, full, and waning phases of the Moon.

The diagram on page 16 shows the twelve signs arranged in

their sequence round the zodiac. Notice how cleverly the cycle and phases interweave:

(a) Outgoing and collecting energies alternate, with no two the same next to each other;

(b) Physical ebb and flow are followed by mental ebb and flow alternately in pairs round the circle, meaning that the elements follow in sequence round the circle three times;

(c) Cardinal, fixed, and mutable qualities follow in sequence round the circle four times, and yet

(d) No two elements or qualities the same are next to each other, even though their sequences are not broken.

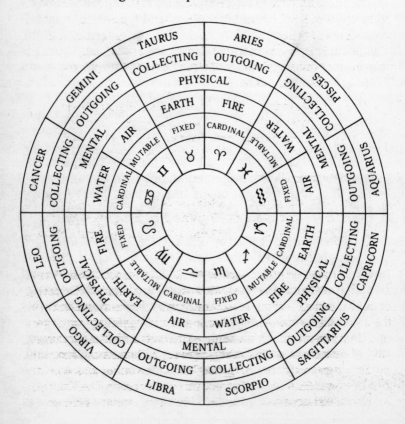

The interweaving is perfect. The zodiac shows all forms of energy, physical and mental, outgoing or incoming, waxing or waning, harmoniously forming a perfectly balanced unity when all the components are taken together. Humanity, as a whole, contains all the possibilities; each individual is a component necessary to the whole.

All this can be a bit long-winded when what you want is some way of holding all that information for instant recall and use, which is where the nine words come in.

If a single word is used for the kind of energy flow, and another two for the element and quality, then they can be used to form a sentence which will describe the way the energy is being used.

As a suggestion (use other words if they are more meaningful to you), try 'outgoing' and 'collecting' for the energy flows.

Next, for the elements:

Fire	:	activity	(Aries, Leo, Sagittarius)
Earth	:	material	(Taurus, Virgo, Capricorn)
Air	:	communication	(Gemini, Libra, Aquarius)
Water	:	feelings	(Cancer, Scorpio, Pisces)

And for the qualities:

Cardinal	:	defining	(Aries, Cancer, Libra, Capricorn)
Fixed	:	maintaining	(Taurus, Leo, Scorpio, Aquarius)
Mutable	:	using	(Gemini, Virgo, Sagittarius, Pisces)

Now in answer to the question 'What is a Gemini doing?' and answer can be formed as 'He's outgoing, and he's using communication', which neatly encapsulates the motivation of the sign. All that you need to know about the guiding principles of a Gemini individual, no matter who he is, is in that sentence. He will never deviate from that purpose, and you can adapt your own actions to partner or oppose his intention as you please.

A Scorpio? He's collecting, and he's maintaining his feelings. An Arian? He's outgoing, and he's defining activity. And so on.

Those nine words, or some similar ones which you like better, can be used to form effective and useful phrases which describe the motivation of everybody you will ever meet. How different people show it is their business, but their motivation and purpose is clear if you know their birthday.

Remember, too, that this motivation works at all levels, from the immediate to the eternal. The way a Taurean conducts himself in today's problems is a miniature of the way he is trying to achieve his medium-term ambitions over the next two or three years. It is also a miniature of his whole existence: when, as an old man, he looks back to see what he tried to do and what he achieved, both the efforts and the achievement, whatever it is, can be described in the same phrase with the same three words.

2. The Planets and the Horseshoe

You will have heard, or read, about the planets in an astrological context. You may have a horoscope in a magazine which says that Mars is here or Jupiter is there, and that as a consequence this or that is likely to happen to you. Two questions immediately spring to mind: What do the planets signify? How does that affect an individual?

The theory is straightforward again, and not as complex as that of the zodiac signs in the previous chapter. Remember that the basic theory of astrology is that since the universe and mankind are part of the same Creation, they both move in a similar fashion, so Man's movements mirror those of the heavens. So far, so good. If you look at the sky, night after night, or indeed day after day, it looks pretty much the same; the stars don't move much in relationship to each other, at least not enough to notice. What do move, though, are the Sun and Moon, and five other points of light—the planets. It must therefore follow that if these are the things which move, they must be the things which can be related to the movements of Man. Perhaps, the theory goes, they have areas of the sky in which they feel more at home, where the energy that they represent is stronger; there might be other places where they are uncomfortable and weak, corresponding to the times in your life when you just can't win no matter what you do. The planets would then behave like ludo counters, moving round the heavens trying to get back to a home of their own colour, and then starting a new game.

The scheme sounds plausible, makes a sort of common sense, and is endearingly human; all hallmarks of astrological thought, which unlike scientific thought has to relate everything to the human experience. And so it is: the planets are given values to show the universal energy in different forms, and given signs of the zodiac as homes. Therefore your Sun sign also has a planet to look after it, and the nature of that planet will show itself strongly in your character.

The planets used are the Sun and Moon, which aren't really planets at all, one being a satellite and the other a star, and then Mercury, Venus, Mars, Jupiter, and Saturn. This was enough until the eighteenth century, when Uranus was discovered, followed in the subsequent two hundred years by Neptune and Pluto. Some modern astrologers put the three new planets into horoscopes, but it really isn't necessary, and may not be such a good idea anyway. There are three good reasons for this:

(a) The modern planets break up the symmetry of the original system, which was perfectly harmonious;

(b) The old system is still good enough to describe everything that can happen in a human life, and the modern planets have little to add;

(c) Astrology is about the relationship between the sky and a human being. An ordinary human being cannot see the outer planets on his own; he needs a telescope. We should leave out of the system such things as are of an extra-human scale or magnitude: they do not apply to an ordinary human. If we put in things which are beyond ordinary human capabilities, we cannot relate them to the human experience, and we are wasting our time.

In the diagram on page 21, the zodiac is presented in its usual form, but it has also been split into two from the start of Leo to the start of Aquarius. The right hand half is called the solar half, and the other one is the lunar half. The Sun is assigned to Leo because in the Northern hemisphere, where astrology started, August is when you feel the influence of the Sun most, especially in the Eastern Mediterranean, where the Greeks and the other early Western civilizations were busy putting the framework of astrology together in the second millennium BC. The Sun is important because it gives light. The Moon gives light too; it is reflected sunlight, but it is enough to see by, and this is enough to give the Sun and Moon the title of 'the Lights' in astrology. The Moon is assigned to Cancer, so that the two of them can balance and complement each other. From there, moving away from the Lights around the circle on both sides, the signs have the planets assigned to them starting with the fastest mover, Mercury, and continuing in decreasing order of speed. Saturn is the slowest mover of all, and the two signs opposite to the Lights are both governed by that planet. The reasons for this

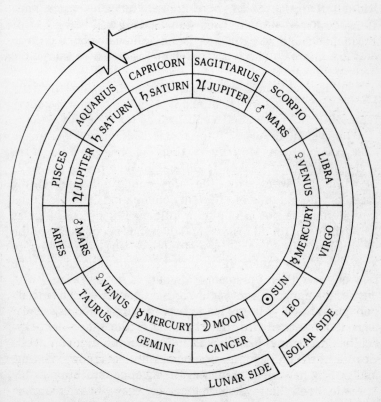

apparent assymmetry will be explained in a little while. This arrangement is, of course, the horseshoe of the title to this chapter.

The Sun and Moon work in a similar fashion to the outgoing and collecting energies we noted earlier with the twelve signs. The Sun is radiant above all else; energy comes outwards from it, warming and energizing all those around it. Leo people, whose sign is the Sun's, work like this by being at the centre of a group of people and acting as inspiration and encouragement to them all. The Moon reflects the Sun's light, and energies of a lunar kind are directed inwards towards the core of the person. The two energies are necessarily linked; lunar people would starve without the solar folks' warmth, but the solar types need someone to radiate to or their purpose is unfulfilled.

The planets on each side of the horseshoe display their own energies in a solar or lunar way depending on which side of the pattern they are on.

Mercury and Venus form a pair, representing complementary but opposite ideas, which should be familiar by now. Mercury represents difference, and Venus stands for similarity.

Wherever anything new forms that is distinguishable from the background, then Mercury is there making it what it is, highlighting what makes it different. Anything separate is Mercurial, and words, since they are separate and can be strung together into millions of different combinations, are Mercurial too. Mercury is not a long-term influence; it notes things as being different for an instant, and then they become part of the establishment, and something else is new elsewhere. Because 'new' is an instantaneous state—that is, something can only be new once, and for a moment—Mercury is not associated with anything lasting, and its rapid motion as a planet leads to its being associated with the idea of speed. Virgo, Mercury's solar sign, is concerned with the changing of the shape of things ('collecting, using material' in our keyword system), while Gemini, the lunar sign, is concerned with reading and writing, and getting new ideas ('outgoing, using communication').

Venus does the reverse; it looks for that which is similar,

finding points of contact to make relationships between common interests and energies. It likes to preserve the harmonies of life, and resents anything which might interrupt them. Love and affection are naturally Venusian, but so is music and all of the Arts, for the harmonies they contain. Expressed in a solar way, Venus is Libra, the maker of relationships; its lunar face is Taurus, emphasizing food and furnishings as things which give pleasure to the individual.

The next pair are Mars and Jupiter. Mars applies force from the outside to impose structure on a disordered universe, while Jupiter expands forcibly from the inside to give growth and wealth, inviting everyone else to join in.

Mars is pure force, energy in a straight line with a direction to go in. Anger and passion are both Martian, and so is lust, because they are all examples of great energy directed towards a given end. Note that Martian force is not necessarily strength, wealth, or know-how, just pure energy, which often boils over and needs controlling. Mars is the power in an athlete, and in an assassin too. It is also the power in a lover, because the urge to create is also the urge to pro-create, and if that energy fulfils its purpose then that creation takes place. Scorpio is its solar side, the power to control and create; in lunar form it is shown by Aries, as energy enjoyed for its own sake by its owner, with no purpose except to express it.

Jupiter is the spirit of expansion from within; not only does it oppose Mars' force from outside, it opposes Mars' physicality with its own mental emphasis. Jupiter develops the mind, then. As it does so, it develops all natural talents of an academic nature, and encourages movement, enquiry and travel to broaden experience and knowledge. The Solar expression of this is Sagittarius, where the centaur symbol is both a wise teacher and a free-roaming wild horse at the same time. Jupiter in a lunar sense is Pisces, where the imagination is developed to a greater extent than anywhere else, but used to provide an internal dream world for the owner's pleasure. Great sensitivity here, but the lunar energies are not of the sort to be expressed; rather other energies are *im*pressed on the Piscean mind.

Saturn is the last of the five planets. He stands alone, and if it is necessary to consider him as paired with anything it is with the Lights as an entity together. The Lights are at the centre of the system; Saturn is at its edge. They are the originators of the energies of the zodiac, and he is the terminator. Everything to do with limits and ends is his. He represents Time, and lots of it, in contrast to Mercury, which represented the instant. He represents the sum total of all things, and the great structures and frameworks of long-term endeavour. In solar form he is Capricorn, the representative of hard work, all hierarchies, and all rulers; in lunar form he is Aquarius, showing the horizontal structure of groups of people within society at different levels. Here he denies the activity of Mars, because society is too big for one person to change against the collective will, and he contains the expansion of Jupiter within himself. Venus and Mercury can neither relate to it nor make it change, because it is always the same, in the end.

The planets show important principles in action, the same as the zodiac does. You have probably noticed that the horseshoe of the planets and the ring of the zodiac say the same thing in a different way, and that is true about most things in astrology. It may be that the two systems interrelate and overlap because they are from the same source: after all, $3+2+2=7$, which is the planet's total, and $3 \times 2 \times 2=12$, which is the signs'. How you assign the elements and qualities, pairs of planets and lights is for you to decide. The joy of astrology, like all magic, is that it has you at the centre, and is made to fit its user's requirements. Now you know the principles, you can use it as you please, and as it seems relevant to you.

Part 2

Yourself—and Others

3. The Essential Sagittarius

All the energy in the zodiac is solar, but that solar energy takes many forms. It is moderated and distributed through the planetary energies until it finally shows in you, the individual. As a Sagittarius, the prime planetary energy is that of Jupiter; you will be motivated by, and behave in the manner of, the energies of Jupiter. To remind yourself of what that means, read the section on Jupiter on page 23. As a sign of the zodiac, Sagittarius is a Mutable Fire sign. Remind yourself what that means by reading page 17. Now we have to see how those essential principles work when expressed through a person and his motivation.

What it Means to be a Sagittarius

You know what it is to be a Sagittarius, because you are one; but you probably don't know what it is that makes a Sagittarius the way he is, because you cannot stand outside yourself. You would have to be each of the other eleven signs in turn to understand the nature of the energy that motivates you. This essential energy is in every Sagittarian, but it shows itself to different extents and in different ways. Because it is in every single Sagittarian, it is universal rather than specific, and universal ideas tend to come in language which sounds a little on the woolly side. You will think that it isn't really about what makes you who you are, because you don't feel like that every day—or at least you think you don't. In fact, you feel like that all the time, but you don't notice it any more than you notice your eyes focusing, yet they do it all the time, and you see things the way you do because of it.

The first thing to note is that the zodiac is a circle, not a line with a beginning and an end. If it were a line, then Sagittarius would be three-quarters of the way along it, but that would be to miss the point; if the zodiac is a circle, then Sagittarius is a stage in an endlessly repeating cycle, and we will get a much better idea of what it is if we look to see where it came from, and where it is going.

The sign before Sagittarius is Scorpio. Scorpio represents the individual maintaining control over everything and everybody he comes in contact with. To a Scorpio, if there is no control, the value of things might be wasted and lost; there is also the possibility that the Scorpio himself might be put at risk if he were to let too much slip. There must come a time, though, when he is completely sure of himslf, and knows that he is strong enough to resist most of what the world can throw at him. He will have acquired a great deal of knowledge and information—too much, in fact, to keep to himself. The only thing he can do, then, is to give some of it out again. This is the next stage in the cycle—Sagittarius.

Sagittarius has confidence in his own abilities; even if he has not met a particular problem before, he is sure that he can resolve it somehow, and equally sure that it is unlikely to injure him in any lasting way. He transfers his confidence to others, by telling them what he knows, in the belief that they will be the same as he is once they have been taught. The end result of his being so useful to society is that his reputation is increased; if that increase in reputation were to be translated into measurable quantities, such as being appointed to some prestigious post, or being paid large amounts of money for his knowledgeable advice, then he would have reached yet another stage in the cycle, that of Capricorn. For the moment, though, we must stay with Sagittarius—a strange mixture of curiosity, knowledge, and blind optimism, a creature who is eager to show what he can do, but who seldom considers being paid for it.

Sagittarius is the last of the Fire signs, the final version of that creative force which is so athletically displayed in the Arian, and so warm and cheerful in the Leo. A Sagittarian is a little of both of these, and more besides. Aries uses his energy for direct physical action; he decides on a course of action, and goes to it at once. Unless he is actually doing something, he is unhappy. Sagittarius works in a similar way, but his preferred work area is that of ideas in social context. He likes to know what everybody else knows. He likes to hear everybody else's opinion. He can see at once what they really mean, even if that's not what they actually say, and he will tell them so—at once, face to face. Direct, open, perceptive, inquisitive; this is Fire energy at work in the world of ideas and beliefs. What it is looking for is truth; it will burn away anything which has been built up to obscure or disguise the truth, until the essence of the argument stands there naked for all to see. Notice how similar Aries and Sagittarius are; one is a physical energy, and the other is an intellectual energy, but they share the qualities of Fire—they are effective, direct, and pure.

That piercing flame has already made the Sagittarian well aware of what he is; he knows all his own motives, and he is honest with himself. He has nothing to fear, either from himself or from anybody else, and he knows it. Because of this, he can be honest all the time, and he is. There are social disadvantages to being both absolutely honest and accurately perceptive at the same time, although the Sagittarian will not see them; to him, it is the only way to be. His friends bear the scars of his wounding remarks, but they forgive him because they can see that he really is as honest as he says he is, and he has no malice in him. He is only concerned with the truth that lies at the heart of things. Scorpios often dig down to the heart of things, too, but what they want is the answer, not the truth; they are very different things.

Sagittarius does not just acquire truth for its own sake, collecting it like something antique and valuable. He is a Mutable sign, and that means he wants to use things. In his case, he wants to use what he knows to be true, distributing the ideas to as large an audience as possible, so that everybody can put them into action, and so produce real results to the benefit of all. It all sounds very noble, and for the most part it is; but as any Sagittarian will immediately see, it gives the Sagittarian what he wants at the same time. As the ideas circulate, they change: they mutate, in fact. This is what a mutable sign needs to see— change, providing him with new combinations to examine all the time, nothing ever quite the same twice.

Sagittarius is ruled by Jupiter, and it is this which drives the Sagittarian to seek ever wider horizons. Sagittarius is the only Fire sign ruled by a planet whose energies are those of outward movement. The combination of Fire and expansiveness produces an irrepressible optimism; the outlook must always be onwards, outwards, and upwards. Looking inwards, downwards, or back is something a Sagittarian finds most unnatural, and he cannot really understand why many people do.

Each zodiac sign has a part of the body associated with it, and somebody born under that sign will find that their life is led in a way parallel to the action of that part of the body. In the case of Sagittarius that part of the body is the thighs. Here are the biggest muscles in the body, the ones used when you run and jump. Mobility is very important to Sagittarians; when they stop moving, they are ill at ease. It is their enjoyment of movement, coupled with the sense of fun they get from Jupiter, which leads to them being described as 'sports-loving' in many astrology books. Mobility combines activity with change of circumstances, which is what the sign really needs.

Sagittarians jump in a figurative sense, too: they jump from one idea to another. They are capable of enormous leaps of imagination and perception; there is no idea or concept that they cannot master, and they love coming across a new one, especially if it influences a large number of people. For this reason, Sagittarians are often very interested in the Law or organized religion; in both cases they are able to deal with a large body of ideas that influence a great number of people.

Finally, Sagittarians jump in the popular sense, as well. They have simple but strong sexual appetites, and are usually very attractive sexually. Many find it difficult to reconcile the intellectualism of the sign with its basic sexual nature, and often conclude that the intellectual side must be some sort of a pretence. It is not so: what is happening is that the Sagittarian is trying to express his own energy, and to give himself to others in a way that will have some sort of a useful result. All the Fire signs are like this.

Sagittarius does have two sides to him, in any case. A look at the symbol of the sign is often useful, and in this case it is particularly illuminating. The centaur has the top half of a man, and the bottom half of a horse; the mixture of the intellectual and the animal is there for all to see. Notice also the fact that the Sagittarian centaur is an archer; his arrows are his piercing intellect, shot into the sky to symbolize his interest in higher ideals, such as Truth. He has no idea where the arrows fall, and he doesn't care; he has plenty more where they came from. He has four hooves; they carry him further, and faster, than the feet of ordinary men, but they also mean that he will kick if he is tied down or denied movement. And last, but not least, there is something about a horse, at least in the popular imagination, which makes you want to stroke it, talk to it, and feel reassured by its presence. A Sagittarian is a horse which can talk back.

Early, Middle or Late? The Decanates

Each of the zodiac signs is divided into degrees, like an arc of any other circle. Since a circle has 360 degrees, then each sign must be 30 degrees, since there are twelve signs. Each of the signs is further split into sections of ten degrees, called decanates. There are three decanates in each sign, and the one that your birthday falls in will tell you a little more about how that Sagittarian energy actually works in you as an individual.

First decanate (22 November-1 December)
This is the purest form of Sagittarius. There is a double helping of Jupiter's energy here, expressed as a mind interested in matters on the largest and most far-reaching scales possible.

Religion is assigned to this part of the sign, not in its role as a personal faith, but as the beliefs held by great numbers of people. All beliefs, including every kind of moral philosophy, are here. Do you have very strong views on things, a set of guiding principles that shape your opinions? All legal processes in an abstract sense are here; that is to say, the Law rather than the judge. There are a very great number of Sagittarian lawyers, though it is hard to say whether they do it from a belief in justice or from love of a clever argument. All things which are to do with looking upwards and outwards are here, such as astronomy, and probably astrology too; clairvoyance, a product of far-reaching thought if ever there was one, is in this section of the sign too. Are these the sort of things you feel an affinity with? If not, perhaps you are more interested in straightforward commercial life, though even there you cannot resist the double Jupiter influence. Foreign trade, as opposed to local or domestic, is given to this part of the sign. Whatever you do, you will find yourself drawn to the far-reaching or the distant qualities of things if this is your decanate.

Second decanate (2–11 December)

Jupiter's expansive influence here is concentrated and given purpose by the influence of Mars; these Sagittarians are much more concerned to see definite results for their efforts. The first decanate was happy to consider philisophy for its own sake, almost, but this one wants to do something with it, and its concerns are much more down to earth. Mars gives a need for physical involvement, wherever he is found; and so in the case of the Sagittarian he will redirect the need to explore new things down onto a physical level and away from the mental and spiritual one. The people of this decanate are the travellers and explorers; Mars and Jupiter keep them hungry for new places to see, new roads to travel, new people to meet and languages to speak. All sorts of exploration and adventure find themselves assigned to this part of the sign; air travel and sea voyages are here too, because they are usually over long distances and involve some degree of risk (Mars for danger, Jupiter for confidence). If your birthday is here, you probably like travelling for its own sake, and would willingly go anywhere just for the experience, especially if the means of transport were itself interesting or unusual.

Third decanate (12-21 December)
The final decanate sees the expansiveness of Jupiter allied to the warmth of the Sun: an excellent combination, but one that limits the sense of movement normally found in the sign. The energy of the individual in this case is not devoted to grand ideals as in the first decanate, nor physical experience, as in the second, but to individual mental development. People with their birthdays here think very carefully about things. They come to personal conclusions rather than general ones, and are often entirely original in their thinking. Inventions and scientific thinking are attributed to this part of the sign, but so are acts of faith, and mysticism; they don't sound as though they have a lot in common, but if you think for a few moments you will see that they are all products of deep thought on an individual level, applied to universal themes. The development of ideas is a Sagittarian process; this section of the sign specializes in it. The movement and exchange of argument, so easy to see in other Sagittarians, is conducted internally in the people of this decanate. They may be less noisy than the other Sagittarians, but they are still searching for the truth just the same.

Three Phases of Life: Sagittarius as Child, Adult, Parent

The Sagittarian Child
Sagittarian children are wise beyond their years, and often behave like little adults; Sagittarian adults, though, are eternal children. How does this come about? It is to do with Jupiter, as you might expect. This big planet gives a bouncy energy and a sense of inquisitive adventurousness to the young Sagittarian, and this is seen as a good thing by his parents. He will always be

asking 'Why?', and wanting a better explanation than 'because they are, that's why'. His attention span isn't very long, but it isn't because he can't concentrate; on the contrary, it is because he understands the essence of things very quickly indeed, and is eager to learn something else as well. To this child, the world is full of new and interesting things, and each one captivates him completely—for a few minutes. Of course, these traits are not going to vanish overnight; once a Sagittarian, always a Sagittarian. Consequently the fascination, the curiosity, and the delight in new discovery is there in the adult too: hence the 'eternal child' epithet.

The clear perception of the real reasons for things which is part of the Sagittarian character is considered a valuable talent in an adult, but somewhat precocious in a child. When told by his parents not to play by the river, the Sagittarian child knows at once that what they really mean is that they are frightened lest he fall in and drown. Since he knows that he will be careful, and knows that the river could be dangerous, he feels that he need not take his parents' warning literally. When he is later punished for disobedience, he explains his thinking, but is not taken seriously. The same happens at school, and with his friends: he will have to wait until he is considerably older before his perceptive mind is given the credit for being what it is.

The Sagittarian Adult

Most people from the other eleven signs find Sagittarians easy to understand, or so they think. In fact, they have usually *mis*understood. The six 'collecting' signs (page 12) are quite convinced that the Sagittarian's optimism is some enormous confidence trick, and that underneath there is some shy and frightened animal nearly dead from worry. It must be the case, they say: how can a single person have all that energy and confidence otherwise? Nobody said anything about the zodiac being fair; it is balanced, when taken as a whole, but individual sections of it needn't be particularly fair, and they aren't. Sagittarians have confidence, imagination, optimism, and luck, and they're not making any of it up, either. So how come, say the other eleven signs, and probably a few Sagittarians as well this time, that with all that going for them, Sagittarians aren't more successful?

Easy. They give it all away. To know a thing is enough for a Sagittarian; actually doing it isn't interesting, unless in doing it he can show it to somebody else, and they can then do it for themselves. They are teachers, discoverers, thinkers; not workers, hoarders, or bankers. 'Success' is a material thing, described in Capricorn/Taurus, Earth element terms: how can a Fire element person find that attractive? Besides, success means responsibility, and responsibilities tie you down; a Sagittarian wouldn't allow that to happen. Freedom of movement means more to him than a big pay cheque, and the trappings of success are too heavy to travel with; they don't permit flexibility or change—more Sagittarian essentials.

Sagittarians already know more than most people can ever imagine learning; they can see in an instant what it takes many people years to see. They are never upset by obstacles, and bounce back after the most crushing setbacks as though nothing has happened. In addition, they are genuinely lucky. None of this matters to them; what matters is that they are not tied down, and that they can put their enormous knowledge to general use. No wonder the other eleven signs don't understand them.

The Sagittarian Parent
Being a parent is a natural thing for a Sagittarian. For a start, they have the child's vision of the world, where everything is new and interesting, and they never lose it. They are also natural teachers; when a child wants to know why something is the way it is, the Sagittarian parent knows the answer, and is delighted to be asked. Sometimes he doesn't even need to be asked—and sometimes even the most inquisitive child can find the constant flow of answers more than he really wants! Sagittarians see the job of being a parent as one of talking, teaching, and playing— and they love doing all three. The idea of the responsibility of parenthood, or of an investment in the future, isn't really Sagittarian, nor is the idea of instilling a sense of discipline and

duty into the child. Here is the drawback to the Sagittarian approach: they have little regard for rules and formal behaviour themselves, and so it never occurs to them to instill it in their children. Like father, like son, really.

4. Sagittarian Relationships

How Zodiacal Relationships Work

You might think that relationships between two people, described in terms of their zodiac signs, might come in 144 varieties; that is, twelve possible partners for each of the twelve signs. The whole business is a lot simpler than that. There are only seven varieties of relationship, although each of those has two people in it, of course, and the role you play depends on which end of the relationship you are at.

You may well have read before about how you are supposed to be suited to one particular sign or another. The truth is usually different. Sagittarians are supposed to get on with Arians and Leos, and indeed they do, for the most part, but it is no use reading that if you have always found yourself attracted to Cancerians, is it? There has to be a reason why you keep finding Cancerians attractive, and it is not always to do with your Sun sign; other factors in your horoscope will have a lot to do with it. The reason you prefer people of certain signs as friends or partners is because the relationship of your sign to theirs produces the sort of qualities you are looking for, the sort of behaviour you find satisfactory. When you have identified which of the seven types of basic relationship it is, you can see which signs will produce that along with your own, and then read the motivation behind it explained later on in more detail in

'The Sagittarian Approach to Relationships' and the individual compatibility sections.

Look at the diagram on page 16. All you have to do is see how far away from you round the zodiacal circle your partner's Sun sign is. If they are Taurus, they are five signs in front of you. You are also, of course, five signs behind them, which is also important, as you will see in a little while. If they are Virgo, they are three signs behind you, and you are three signs in front of them. There are seven possibilities: you can be anything up to six signs apart, or you can both be of the same sign.

Here are the patterns of behaviour for the seven relationship types.

Same sign

Somebody who is of the same sign as you acts in the same way that you do, and is trying to achieve the same result for himself. If your goals permit two winners, this is fine, but if only one of you can be on top, you will argue. No matter how temperamental, stubborn, devious, or critical you can be, they can be just the same, and it may not be possible for you to take the same kind of punishment you hand out to others. In addition, they will display every quality which really annoys you about yourself, so that you are constantly reminded of it in yourself as well as in them. Essentially, you are fighting for the same space, and the amount of tolerance you have is the determining factor in the survival of this relationship.

One sign apart

Someone one sign forward from you acts as an environment for you to grow in. In time, you will take on those qualities yourself. When you have new ideas, they can often provide the encouragement to put them into practice, and seem to have all your requirements easily available. Often, it is this feeling that they already know all the pitfalls that you are struggling over which can be annoying; they always seem to be one step ahead of you, and can seemingly do without effort all the things which you have to sweat to achieve. If the relationship works well, they are helpful to you, but there can be bitterness and jealousy if it doesn't.

Someone one sign back from you can act as a retreat from the pressures of the world. They seem to understand your particular needs for rest and recovery, whatever they may be, and can usually provide them. They can hold and understand your innermost secrets and fears; indeed, their mind works best with the things you fear most, and the fact that they can handle these so easily is a great help to you. If the relationship is going through a bad patch, their role as controller of your fears gets worrying, and you will feel unnerved in their presence, as though they were in control of you. When things are good, you feel secure with them behind you.

Two signs apart
Someone two signs forward from you acts like a brother or sister. They are great friends, and you feel equals in each other's company; there is no hint of the parent-child or master-servant relationship. They encourage you to talk, even if you are reticent in most other company; the most frequently heard description of these relationships is 'We make each other laugh'. Such a partner can always help you put into words the things that you want to say, and is there to help you say them. This is the relationship that teenagers enjoy with their 'best friend'. There is love, but it does not usually take sexual form, because both partners know that it would spoil the relationship by adding an element of unnecessary depth and weight.

Someone two signs behind you is a good friend and companion, but not as intimate as somebody two signs forward. They are the sort of people you love to meet socially; they are reliable and honest, but not so close that things become suffocatingly intense. They stop you getting too serious about life, and turn your thoughts outwards instead of inwards, involving you with other people. They stop you from being too selfish, and help you give the best of yourself to others. This relationship, then, has a cool end and a warm end; the leading sign feels much closer to his partner than the trailing sign does, but they are both satisfied by the relationship. They particularly value its chatty quality, the fact that it works even better when in a group, and its tone of affection and endearment rather than passion and obsession.

Three signs apart

Someone three signs in front of you represents a challenge of some kind or another. The energies of the pair of you can never run parallel, and so must meet at some time or another. Not head on, but across each other, and out of this you can both make something strong and well established which will serve the two of you as a firm base for the future. You will be surprised to find how fiercely this person will fight on your behalf, or for your protection; you may not think you need it, and you will be surprised that anybody would think of doing it, but it is so nonetheless.

Someone three signs behind you is also a challenge, and for the same reasons as stated above; from this end of the relationship, though, they will help you achieve the very best you are capable of in a material sense. They will see to it that you receive all the credit that is due to you for your efforts, and that everyone thinks well of you. Your reputation is their business, and they will do things with it that you could never manage yourself. It's like having your own P.R. team. This relationship works hard, gets results, and makes sure the world knows it. It also looks after itself, but it needs a lot of effort putting in.

Four signs apart

Someone four signs forward from you is the expression of yourself. All the things you wanted to be, however daring, witty, sexy, or whatever, they already are, and you can watch them doing it. They can also help you to be these things. They do things which you think are risky, and seem to get away with them. There are things you aim towards, sometimes a way of life that you would like to have, which these people seem to be able to live all the time; it doesn't seem to worry them that things might go wrong. There are lots of things in their life which frighten you, which you would lie awake at nights worrying about, which they accept with a child's trust, and which never go wrong for them. You wish you could be like that.

Someone four signs behind you is an inspiration to you. All the things you wish you knew, they know already. They seem so wise and experienced, and you feel such an amateur; luckily, they are kind and caring teachers. They are convincing, too. When they speak, you listen and believe. It's nice to know there's somebody there with all the answers. This extraordinary relationship often functions as a mutual admiration society, with each end wishing it could be more like the other; unfortunately, it is far less productive than the three-sign separation, and much of its promise remains unfulfilled. Laziness is one of the inherent qualities of a four-sign separation; all its energies are fulfilled, and it rarely looks outside itself for something to act upon. Perhaps this is just as well for the rest of us.

Five signs apart
Someone five signs ahead of you is your technique. You know what you want to do; this person knows how to do it. He can find ways and means for you to do what you want to be involved in, and he can watch you while you learn and correct your mistakes. They know the right way to go about things, and have the clarity of thought and analytical approach necessary if you are to get things clear in your mind before you get started

Someone five signs behind you is your resource. Whenever you run out of impetus or energy, they step forward and support you. When you're broke, they lend you money, and seldom want it returned. When you need a steadying hand because you think you've over-reached yourself, they provide it. All this they do because they know that it's in their best interest as well as yours, to help you do things, and to provide the material for you to work with. You can always rely on them for help, and it's nice to know they will always be there. They cannot use all their talent on their own; they need you to show them how it should be done. Between you, you will use all that you both have to offer effectively and fully, but it is a relationship of cooperation and giving; not all the zodiac signs can make it work well enough.

Six signs apart

Someone six signs apart from you, either forwards or backwards, is both opponent and partner at the same time. You are both essentially concerned with the same area of life, and have the same priorities. Yet you both approach your common interests from opposite directions, and hope to use them in opposite ways. Where one is private, the other is public, and where one is self-centred, the other shares himself cheerfully. The failings in your own make-up are complemented by the strengths in the other; it is as if, between you, you make one whole person with a complete set of talents and capabilities. The problem with this partnership is that your complementary talents focus the pair of you on a single area of life, and this makes for not only a narrow outlook, but also a lack of flexibility in your response to changes. If the two of you are seeing everything in terms of career, or property, or personal freedom, or whatever, then you will have no way to deal effectively with a situation which cannot be dealt with in those terms. Life becomes like a seesaw; it alternates which end it has up or down, and can sometimes stay in balance; but it cannot swing round to face another way, and it is fixed to the ground so that it does not move.

These are the only combinations available, and all partnerships between two people can be described as a version of one of the seven types. It must be remembered, though, that some of the roles engendered by these dispositions of sign to sign are almost impossible to fulfil for some of the signs, because their essential energies, and the directions they are forced to take by the planets behind them, drive them in ways which make it too difficult. To form a relationship based on sharing and acceptance is one thing: to do it when you are governed by a planet like Mars is somethings else. Even when the relationship can form, the sort of approach produced by, say, Jupiter, is a very different thing from that produced by Venus.

The next thing you must consider, then, is how you, as a Sagittarius, attempt relationships as a whole, and what you try to find in them. Then you must lay the qualities and outlook of each of the twelve signs over the roles they must play in the seven relationship types, and see whether the pair of you manage to make the best of that relationship, or not.

The seven relationship types are common to all the signs, relating to all the other signs. You can use your understanding of them to analyse and understand the relationship between any pair of people that you know, whether or not they are Sagittarius; but to see how the characters fit into the framework in more detail, you will need to look at the individual compatibilities, of which just the Sagittarius ones are given in this book.

The Sagittarius Approach to Relationships

A relationship is usually formed when two people find that what they have to offer, and what they want in return, are mutually compatible. Sagittarians are unusual in that they have plenty to offer, and don't seem to need a lot in return. Although that isn't entirely true, as we will see in a little while, it is a good enough general rule.

Sagittarians like yourself don't need a partner as a comforter, because you seldom feel that the world is too hard on you; nor do you need one as a protector, because you don't feel threatened or oppressed. You don't want a partner to be a stabilizing influence, because you'd rather not be in a rut, and you don't need one to cheer you up and inspire you either, because you are already happy and creative. You don't need caring for, because you can get yourself out of anything you get yourself into, and you don't want anybody you have to care for, because that would limit your freedom. What you want is a playmate.

It is a difficult thing to find, and a difficult thing for other people to understand. You are more than willing to give your time and talent to anyone who will appreciate them, but at no time must you be made to feel that you *have* to give them. When that happens, you sense dependence, permanence, and commitment beginning to form, and that sets the alarm bells ringing inside your head. Time to move on, you think. As long as the other person enjoys your company, but is quite capable of pursuing his own interests in your absence, then you are happy to have him around, provided of course that you enjoy his company too.

Hierarchy is an idea which you don't much like. It is quite possible to have a hierarchy with only two people, of course: one is the dominant partner, and the other allows himself to be led. Quite a number of zodiac signs are willing to be led; it takes away the responsibility of decision-making, and gives the security of knowing that somebody is looking after your interests for you. That's not your style at all – you take your own decisions, and you don't like being told what to do by people who don't know anything like as much as you do, so therefore don't know what they're doing.

Some zodiac signs prefer to be the dominant partner, but that's not your style either. To you, that means that you have to be responsible for them, and to consider their needs as well as your own. That would stop you from chasing off after new and interesting things which cropped up during the day, wouldn't it? It would also stop you doing things which they couldn't, or would rather not, do. Altogether too much of a limitation.

You don't want to be under anyone's thumb, or walk in anyone's shadow—but nor do you want the sort of relationship where your partner follows you dutifully, ten paces behind. What you want is somebody at your side, seeing things as you see them, doing things as you do them, advancing individually but in the same direction—in fact, travelling together. Now *there's* a Sagittarian idea.

Treating everybody as a potential playmate, which you do, sounds a wonderful idea: it is open, unrestricting, and highly egalitarian. You know all this, of course; it is part of why you do it. There are problems, however, when you apply it in real life, and most of them come in one of two categories.

The first problem area is that you refuse to give some people the respect to which their position has accustomed them. Speaking to the managing directors of multinational corporations, whom you have only just met, with the same cheerful banter you use with your greengrocer sometimes causes offence. The same applies to bank managers, bishops, and royalty; as far as you're concerned, they are all the same as your greengrocer, i.e. people. You simply cannot understand how it could be any other way. Now you see why Sagittarians hate formality (they get caught up in protocol, because they can't understand it), and why all the other signs call them tactless.

The second problem area is when people simply aren't as good as you are. People come in all sizes and abilities, and for you to assume that everybody you meet shares your interests, and is as skilled in those areas as you are, is frankly naïve, but you do it nonetheless. The result is usually disappointment. Sometimes you find yourself helping them along, especially if they have the interest but not the ability, and that appeals to the teacher in you—but it also makes you feel responsible for them, and you don't like that.

Why is it that you don't want a formal relationship? What is it that makes you so dislike commitment and responsibility? Why don't you want anybody to tell you what to do?

In a word, Jupiter. Jupiter is movement, expansion, optimism. Once a thing has taken form, or become fixed, it is no longer of Jupiter—it has become limited and static, which is the province of Saturn. Sagittarius tries to avoid this wherever possible. Jupiter doesn't like being tied down, because then it cannot move or expand. A moving, expansive, un-fixed relationship without the weight of responsibility is what you're looking for, and you approach every new acquaintance with the same aim. Why have a relationship at all, you say. A good point; the answer is that you are an outgoing sign, and all outgoing signs need somebody to collect their energy, so that the flow of energy round the zodiac is maintained. In other words, you need an audience of some sort, somebody you can help, teach, and show off to as well, if we are to be honest.

Assuming that you find a playmate, somebody as talented as you are, who doesn't need you, but quite likes you, then how will you deepen the relationship without making it static?

Sexually, of course. Sagittarians, like all Fire signs, have strong sexual drives. They don't have the majesty of the Leo, nor the sheer power of the Arian, but they don't do badly (they do, after all, have the thighs, and indeed the bottom end generally, of a horse), and they are both imaginative and inventive, which the other Fire signs are not. The essential thing about a Sagittarian's sex drive, though, is that to him it is a physical thing, done for fun, a way of saying how pleased you are to be with somebody. The idea of emotional bonding and commitment has no part in it. Most of the other eleven signs are different in this respect, and are very upset by the Sagittarian's refusal to make the relationship permanent. He's honest and loyal enough while the affair's in progress, but he won't make a commitment.

Sex is a creative act to a Sagittarian; you see it as a form of giving, and you hope that something will grow from it. The procreative function of sex is never far from the Sagittarian mind; it is linked with the idea of expansion and potential for growth—not only the idea of the expanding family and the potential for the future, but the expansion of the body during pregnancy, too. Jupiter works on many levels, but always to the same ends.

Marriage isn't impossible for Sagittarians, even if it sounds unlikely. Once you have found a partner as independently-minded as you are, then there is no reason why you should not travel on, side by side, into the sunset for ever. What you don't want your marriage to be is a static arrangement, with formal routines. For you, it must stay moving, or at least make major moves every few years. It must also contain a variety of people, to maintain the movement so dear to you: either a family, or at least a large number of friends. If you can achieve this moving, expanding marriage, with your partner by your side, then all will be well; if you can't, then you feel tied down and trapped, and you will eventually be forced to break away from it to gain the refreshment you need from movement and change.

Individual Compatibilities Sign by Sign

All relationships between the signs work in the ways described earlier in 'How Zodiacal Relationships Work'. In addition to that, descriptions of how a Sagittarian attempts to form a relationship with someone from each of the twelve signs are given below. I have tried to show not what an Aquarius, for example, is like, but what a Sagittarian sees him as, and how he sees you. Each individual Aquarian looks different, of course, but their motivation is the same, and these descriptions are meant to help you understand what you are trying to do with them, and how they are trying to handle you. As usual, the words he and his can be taken to mean she and her, since astrology makes no distinctions in sex here.

Sagittarius-Aries

This is a very good relationship. They think you are bright and interesting, and you think they are dashing and sexy. Both true, of course: you are both Fire signs, and so you see each other in your true colours.

Arians are very active people; they don't function properly unless they are actually doing something. An idea isn't enough for them—it's only the beginning. They are impatient to see what happens to the idea when it is put into action, and so they do exactly that. Only in the performance of the action can they understand the idea, which you ought to think about.

You see them as fantastically energetic, and you are envious of their ability to turn ideas into actions. Because you are a Mutable sign, you are very good at breaking things down to see what can be extracted from them, but you are much less effective in getting things going, especially when you have to start from scratch. You need something to work with. Aries doesn't—all he needs is a direction to go in, and he's away. Where you will turn an idea around in your head for some time, comparing it to other, similar thoughts you might have had, Aries takes the first idea he comes across and races off to put it into action. What's more, he gets it right first time. Whatever an Aries does is active and effective: in other words, it works. A lot of this is to do with his being a Cardinal sign, but whatever it is, you wish that you could do it.

He has his faults, of course. He won't think before he acts, for instance. It may well be that this is because unless he acts he can't think, but it does have a few drawbacks. He also has no sense of time: everything for him has to happen right now, this minute, just as it does for a young child.

He is very self-sustaining, and he is self-centred, too. This means that he is very happy on his own; he doesn't need a partner for support or protection, and he doesn't really think of sharing his time with somebody else. If somebody else wants to be there while he's being active, then that's fine, as long as they don't get in the way, and don't expect him to stop what he's doing to attend to them. This sounds rather selfish, but it is actually self-*centred*. No matter: it appeals very strongly to you, because you know how he feels. It has all the action, freedom, and movement you could wish for, and none of the commitment you are so keen to avoid.

Is it the perfect partnership? No, not quite. It has all the rugby-team mateyness that you could wish for, and you could hardly get a better companion for an adventure, but the Arian can't offer you intellectual stimulation. He knows it, too: that's what he comes to you for.

He sees you as a great source of inspiration. You can see and understand all the things which he can't quite grasp, and you can tell him what they are like. As a young child will bring a book to its grandfather, and ask him what's in it, so the Arian wants the Sagittarian to show him the inner meanings of things, to tell him how things work, and to fire his imagination. He wants to act on every idea you tell him; everything you say gives him something new to do. Between you, you can create real achievements out of your slightest whim, and the idea of that attracts you enormously— but you would also like him to be able to converse and argue with you at your own level, and he just can't do that, no matter how much he would like to.

As friends, you are ideally suited. You will keep each other amused and cheerful, and you will be able to laugh together at a world which seems altogether too set in its ways to go off and try new things, as you both like to do. As lovers, you are equally well aligned—Aries is more physical than you are, and stronger too, but neither of you use sex as a symbol of personal commitment, so you are unlikely to misconstrue each other's intentions. They are simple souls, though, and will not understand your liking for changing partners every so often.

As business partners you will be unbeatable, provided that you have somebody else on hand to take care of the routine work, and to tie up all the details while the pair of you launch yourselves off into yet another new venture.

As a marriage, this pairing will work very well, provided that you realize that you will eventually have to do things their way; that said, you would rather do things in an Arian way than in the way of some of the other signs.

Sagittarius-Taurus

This relationship is very difficult, and yet in real life it seems to struggle along somehow. It may be that the best thing about this relationship is that the ruling planets of the pair of you—Jupiter and Venus respectively—are essentially kind and well meaning in their nature. If they were not, you would end up throwing plates at each other.

Taureans are essentially static people. The very idea of movement bothers them. They are equally disconcerted by the idea of novelty, since that threatens them with the dissolution of their existing way of life. Difficult for you to imagine, isn't it? You couldn't exists without movement and novelty, and the idea of forming a relationship with somebody so opposed to your own way of life seems difficult to comprehend, even for you.

What they are trying to achieve is a stable way of life, where everything is secure, and where every physical need is met. Taureans are very much lovers of home comforts—they measure themselves by the size and comfort of their homes, and by the amount they have in their larders, just as you measure yourself by how clever you are, and how much you know. They are physical where you are intellectual, and they want comfort where you want excitement.

They are very slow to anger, and will endure a great deal of strain and stress before they eventually take steps to rectify the situation.

Their stability and reliability can have a sort of appeal to you; you wouldn't like to be that way yourself, but somebody who represents constant values in a changing world isn't hard to appreciate. At the end of it all, you realize that what they have is what you are trying to achieve; you want things to take shape as a result of your ideas, for your Fire sign energy to become established in the world as Earth sign energy, such as Taurus. You also know that when you shoot one of your Sagittarian archer's arrows into the air, it will eventually fall to Earth. Although Taurus is the end product, by the time you get there, you will no longer be Sagittarian, and that's why you fight shy of it. You appreciate their stability, and you admire the care that they have lavished on their home and possessions, because you know that you just couldn't give that much time to that sort of thing; but you don't want to be part of it.

They see you as somebody who changes their opinions from one moment to the next, and who seems determined to undermine all that they hold dear. Their eventual reaction to you is to ignore you: they see that you are not concerned with the material world in the same way as they are, and so you do not threaten their possessions. You are also not important, for the same reasons; ideas can safely be ignored by Taureans, because what matters to them is material wealth. This infuriates you: you don't mind them not accepting your ideas, but not to be recognized for having ideas of importance in the first place really drives you wild.

Friendship depends to some extent on having parallel, if not identical, viewpoints. Since you have to struggle even to recognize the existence of each other's way of thinking, you are unlikely to be close friends. Should you be lovers, you will find that the Taurean is capable of a tremendous passion, but you will find it more than you want to deal with, because the emotional content is at least as much as the physical; you would like things a little lighter in tone.

If you marry, it is obviously because you want a secure home base, which the Taurean will gladly provide for you. Don't complain if they are unwilling to change as quickly as you would like them to, or if they place constraints on your personal freedom.

As business partners, you are a lot better than you might think: you do the selling, and let them do the buying.

Sagittarius-Gemini

Gemini is the sign opposite to you in the zodiac, and that means that they have all of your talents, but displayed in the opposite way, which you find irritating. They are so like you, but so different—they seem to be interested in the same things and for the same reasons, but they use them in very different ways, and you find yourself wondering why they won't do things the right (i.e. your) way when it would be so easy for them to do so.

They wonder about you in the same way, of course. Had you thought of that?

A Gemini is the only person in the zodiac who could find you dull. While you are reeling from the shock and the insult to your intelligence, think about how much smaller and faster Mercury is than Jupiter. They are quicker on the uptake than you are, and cleverer in their manipulation of words and ideas. They are also faster movers physically, and their hands can do quick little tricks that yours couldn't begin to.

The idea of little tricks is one of the things that bothers you about Geminis. There is always the suspicion that they are somehow less than honest; you, of course, are absolutely straight, so the slightest deviation from that will show in comparison. You are right: Geminis aren't always honest. They're not consciously dishonest, either; the idea of honesty just doesn't apply to them, because their energies are directed towards their own amusement, and not towards public duty. If it amuses them to twist an argument a little for a better effect, then they will do it; similarly, if there is some fun to be had from a little sleight-of-hand, then they will do that, too.

Geminis seem to spend their time accumulating surface knowledge; it annoys you to see them wasting their talent this way, when they could be investigating the higher intellectual pursuits. It does not occur to you, though, that they like doing things their way, that they don't really have your capacity for pure knowledge, and that they can't see why you spend your time with worthy causes when you could make an absolute fortune using your perception commercially.

Essentially, they use their powerful mentality to amuse themselves, while you feel obliged to use yours for the benefit of everyone. Your attitude seems pompous to him; his seems selfish to you.

It must have struck you by now that there is more to forming a relationship than matching mentalities. There is, but in this case it is the area you keep returning to again and again, because it is the single thing which, more than anything else, you pick up on in each other; everything else gets pushed aside.

As friends, you will get along wonderfully; you will be eager to tell each other new things that you have noticed, and your love of news and gossip generally will keep you chatting away for ever. Gemini will have a little fun at your expense from time to time when he thinks that you are being dull, but you will forgive him; in your opinion, being dull is a punishable offence anyway, and you are grateful for his reminders.

As your lover, Gemini will surprise you: he is even lighter in his affections than you are. Not only does he not want to be involved, he doesn't really want things to be excessively physical anyway—he doesn't have half an animal for his sign the way you do. Sometimes you will be left thinking that you could really do with somebody a little more basic in his tastes.

As business partners you will do very well, but neither of you have any time for boring routine work; this could be a problem, as could the fact that neither of you have much tolerance of things going wrong—you would rather be off starting something new than helping an ailing project through a sticky patch.

These two signs work very well when married to each other. It's not a relationship which values stability and wealth, but it will give you what you want: bright conversation, plenty of variety, and a not-too-serious outlook.

Sagittarius-Cancer

This one is as difficult as the Taurean relationship, but in different ways. In the final analysis, it is probably easier, because the Cancerian will change his position more easily than the Taurean; in fact, he is quite keen to make progress, because he is a cardinal sign. The problem with the Taurean was how to match your desire for movement to somebody who was determined to stay static; the problem here is how to match your openness and love of company to somebody who is very shy and reserved.

Cancerians do not live their life on the outside in the way that you do. They are extremely sensitive, and they respond very quickly to the emotional needs of others; understandably, they have to have a mechanism for shutting off this response, or they would become exhausted just by walking down a crowded street. Remember, Sagittarius, that these people absorb energy from others; they don't pump it out like you do. If, then, they absorb, they don't have much of a choice in what they take in; they will have to take what comes. This makes life a much riskier business than it is for a Fire sign like yourself, and they will make very sure that they trust a person first, before they allow themselves to absorb his influence.

When they find that somebody is in need of their care and protection, they respond at once with love and care. You probably wouldn't notice that anybody needed help—it's not easy to feel a lack of energy in somebody when you are youself an energy source. This is how Sagittarians get their reputation for being unsubtle and insensitive; it's not that you don't care, it's that you can't see when care is needed, or how much.

A Cancerian shields and protects—himself, his family, his friends. He responds, too: it's how he acts. Look at that again— Fire signs act of their own accord, but Water signs react to the actions of others. Cancer, because it is governed by the Moon, reacts by reflecting the kind of light you shine at it. Treat a Cancerian harshly, and see how the crab's pincers nip; treat them with kindness, and they will respond with kindness.

A Cancerian will treat you very warily at first. Your ever-changing point of view means that he has continually to reevaluate you, and see whether he needs to change his responses, or perhaps retreat into his shell: his own security comes first, remember. This process takes time. When you have a new enthusiasm which completely captures your imagination and makes you want to devote the rest of your life to it, as is usual for Sagittarians at weekly intervals, the Cancerian is rather slower to react than you would like. He is also decidedly short on enthusiasm, by your standards; he just doesn't have the energy to throw away in the way that you do. He also worries: what is he to do if things don't quite work out? He doesn't have your ability to recover from setbacks in a matter of minutes, you see.

He gasps at your openness, and closes his eyes in fright at the risks you take; on the other hand, he loves your warmth and genuineness, and he finds your eternal optimism very cheering. You tease them for being so cautious, but you appreciate their selfless devotion to the care of their families and friends— higher motives are something you are very aware of, and anyone who displays them, in whatever form, gets your approval. On a selfish level, there is something that they do for you which no other sign can: when one of your imaginative schemes has collapsed, leaving you temporarily floored, they will care for you, and you appreciate that. A friend whose life you brighten when you are up, and who comforts you when you are down, isn't a bad thing at all, and you know that.

As friends, you are an odd couple, but you like each other's company. It's not easy to see why; perhaps it is because they reflect a little of yourself back at you, and that's the kind of audience you like. As lovers, you are a long way apart. They are very emotionally involved, whereas you are not; their enthusiasm also goes in phases, like lunar phases, which will surprise you at first.

Marriage will take some working at for this pair of signs. Cancer is very home-loving, and seeks always to make a safe retreat for himself and his family; Sagittarius wonders what all the fuss is about. You will have to adjust to each other. The same goes for a business partnership; if you handle the marketing, and they handle the financial side, you won't have any problems—

but don't try to tell each other how to do the job!

Sagittarius-Leo
This is the other partnership possible within our own element. Theoretically it should be as much fun as the Aries pairing, but it isn't. It isn't at all bad, and you enjoy each other's company, but the Leo doesn't bring a smile to your face the way an Arian does. He's a bit static, to your way of thinking. He's bright and warm, generous and friendly; but he isn't keen on seeing new things in the same way that you are, and when he travels, he does it surrounded by familiar things, so that he isn't really changing his surroundings at all. He's not a mover like the Arian, and he hasn't got anything like your intellect; what he's got is warmth and generosity, but you have enough of that yourself, and so you don't find his all that remarkable.

The truth of the matter is that he likes you a lot more than you like him. Not that you dislike him particularly; he's optimistic, open, and lively just like you are, and that's more than can be said for most of the other signs, but he doesn't have anything that would make you want to trade places with him. He adores you, though.

What you have that he wants is wisdom. Look at it this way: Aries has physical confidence, an implicit belief in his own body and its capabilities. Leo has enough of that to be going on with, but more importantly he has social confidence—the stuff that makes everybody cluster round him and want to be his friend. Sagittarius has spiritual confidence: it is his soul that is bright and strong, and the Leo finds that desperately desirable. An Arian wants simply to do things; a Leo wants to be recognized for what he is doing. In the Sagittarian's high principles he sees the perfection of his endeavours: action accumulated into experience, wisdom distilled from that experience, then handed on to influence others, and gratefully acknowledged.

Leo is fine as long as he stays where he is, and he knows that. If anything displaces him from the centre of the action, or something new comes along and changes the order of things, he is troubled. How envious he is of your confidence and mobility!

He is confident enough on his own, of course, but only as long as he has people around him; he can't take his achievements along with him the way you can. Leo is expansive and generous, and Aries is mobile, but only Sagittarius is both; Leo would love to be like that.

What he enjoys that you wish you did (but this he can't give you) is everybody's approval and friendship. Everybody loves a Leo, and he loves being generous to his friends in response to that. The process is self-sustaining, and everyone benefits. Not everybody loves a Sagittarian, as you will have learned by now, though they work in the same way; possibly it is because Leos tend to hand out material comforts, whereas Sagittarians hand out truth and knowledge, which don't always go down so well.

As friends, you get along very well, provided that you can slip into the subordinate role necessary for the friendship to continue. Leos like their friends to treat them as important figures; your dislike of pomp and ceremony could be a hindrance here.

As lovers, you will have a lot of fun; Leos are pretty conventional in their tastes, but they are strong, and they like a good time. There will probably be quite a bit of rolling around on the floor—both of your signs are animals, remember.

The drawback about going into business together is that you won't be able to work for somebody who knows less than you do, whereas the Leo won't play if he can't be boss. The same applies to marriage—he has to be the master of the house, and if you don't want that, then don't marry a Leo. He won't want you to go wandering off on your own, either, as you will inevitably feel drawn to do.

Sagittarius-Virgo

Three-signs-apart relationships aren't usually a good idea; not unless you like having rows, anyway. This one is less of a strain than most, because both of you are pretty flexible in your approach to things, and because both of you have a strong sense of doing things for other people's benefit. All this helps the pair of you make the compromises necessary to form a relationship.

The essential problem is one of scale. You have a boundless imagination which needs to roam free, forming great universal concepts and apply them to the whole of mankind; they have very little imagination, and even less time for hypothetical concepts, preferring to concentrate their energies on the actual job in hand and to make sure that every detail of it is attended to. You see things through a telescope, and they see things through a microscope. Quite some problem, as you will appreciate.

What you have in common, and it is worth building on, is an interest in how things work, and how to do things for the best. In their case, the emphasis is on the actual mechanics of the process; to them 'How does it work?' means taking it apart with a screwdriver; to you, it means 'What do people do with it? How does that help them? Why do they want to do that?

It is important that you should not cross over into each other's territory. As partners, you can accomplish a great deal together, with one of you looking after theory and application, and the other one giving time to technique and efficiency. If you start to apply your generalized grasp of things to specific tasks, you will make errors of detail. Similarly, he lacks both the facility to deal with the theoretical instead of the actual, and the scope to handle things on your scale. Don't criticize him for being fussy over details: somebody has to be, and he has a talent for it. It's not your field, so leave him to it. In the same way, you can cheerfully ignore him when he criticizes you for having your head in the clouds.

After a while you will recognize each other for what you are—experts in parallel fields that do not touch or overlap in any way.

Mentally, you are quite different. Both of you like to see the inner states of things, but the Virgo analyses carefully, bit by bit, whereas you grasp the whole thing at once, and perceive its meaning in one go. You are similar but different emotionally, too. Neither of you wants to feel tied down, but in your case that is because of a love of freedom, whereas for the Virgo it is simply that he feels lost with irrational things like emotions, and so tries not to have much to do with them.

As friends, you should be able to understand each other, at

least. You have similar views, but for different reasons, as we have just seen; if you come to an understanding about the difference of scale in your views of life, then you will probably enjoy comparing your experiences. As lovers, you are not really suited. Virgos are too careful altogether; you prefer things to be a bit more boisterous. In any case, the Virgoan doesn't have the energy of the Fire signs, nor any of your sense of exuberant fun.

As business partners, you need a third person. You work on a large and impractical scale, Sagittarius, and Virgo's scale is too small; most things happen in the middle, and who will look after that?

You *can* work together as a marriage, though you will find their small-scale view very frustrating. The necessary technique is for you to attack common problems from different ends in your own ways.

Sagittarius-Libra

The best of the lot, as far as these relationships go. There's more to matching people astrologically than just comparing Sun signs; but having said that, you won't get far if the Sun signs *don't* match, and as far as you're concerned, this is the one to go for.

You like Librans. It's as simple as that. When you have one of your great ideas in your head, they are interested; when you tell them about it, they like listening. They talk back, too, in just the way you would like them to—brightly, with interest and humour. Their attitude is one of optimism, like your own, and they are quite sure that the next thing is going to be even better than the current one, just as you are. They are friendly, too; they positively adore company, and don't like being on their own any more than you do. When you decide that it's time you got up and did something, they ask to come along for the ride, but they don't get in the way; that's just how you like it. They will fall in love with you, which flatters you enormously, but they don't get emotionally dependent on you, and they don't cling. Nor do they get moody or temperamental—in fact they will do almost anything to avoid an argument, and would much rather think about something else instead, preferably something new and entertaining. Just the same as you, in fact. If you were to sit down with pencil and paper, and make a list of all that you wanted in a partner, you wouldn't come up with anything better than a Libran.

You can't find anything wrong with them at all; in fact they are suspiciously well suited to you, and you may wonder why.

To be fair, they are just as pleasant to everybody, because that's how they are; you may have suspected this. On the other hand, not everybody finds their light and friendly outlook on life to their taste; it happens to suit you very well, so you might as well make the most of it.

Librans are Air sign people. They live in a world of thought, speech, and ideas, where what you say is more interesting than what you do, and where nothing lasts for very long. They are also the Cardinal Air sign, so they are the most active and assertive of their element. You, on the other hand, are a Fire sign, which is to do with creative physical activity; but because you are the Mutable Fire sign, your activity tends to have mental rather than a physical emphasis. So you are the sign of mental activity, and they are the sign of active mentality, which is pretty much the same thing. Now you see why you like each other.

They see you as being much more assertive and effective versions of themselves. That same envy you have of the Arian's energy, they have of yours. They also see you as the ideal conversational partner: they love talking, and you never seem to run out of things to say. They like being entertained, and you seem to know so much (their own minds don't hold deep knowledge like yours does).

As friends, you are perfect. You lead your own lives, but in parallel, and you love to tell each other everything that has happened to you. Your conversations can never become heavy: there is always laughter and entertainment in them somewhere. Even after many years, you should be able to note how genuinely *pleased* you are to see each other, and how much you have to say to each other. Arguments just never seem to surface; you are completely sympathetic to each other's point of view.

As lovers, you should be almost ideal. Librans are a bit on the cool side sexually, but they are very friendly, and being a cardinal sign will give them enough strength to match your Fiery power. Neither of you take it too seriously, and both of you like the affair to be flexible and full of variety; these two things alone make it more enjoyable for you both than your other relationships, even if they have more passion.

As business partners, you will dominate. They are your partner, not you theirs, and that means that if you have some areas where you are lazy, they won't fill in the gaps for you: not necessarily a good thing.

If you marry, you should be very content. The Libran will make your day-to-day existence very pleasant indeed, through his talent for making things relaxed and graceful. Neither of you are much good at fighting your way out of tight corners, though, and you may need some of that quality at some stage.

Sagittarius-Scorpio
There are quite a lot of Sagittarians who have relationships with Scorpios. Like everybody else in the zodiac, they are attracted to the intense energy that the Scorpio puts out. With this particular pairing, the Sagittarian finds that the Scorpio is nothing like as much fun as he had hoped, and the Scorpio finds that holding the Sagittarius in check is more trouble than it's worth. Eventually the Centaur, tired of being made to rear up by having the Scorpion under his hooves, takes his quiver and brains the little beast; then he gallops off into the sunset wishing he hadn't been so hasty.

Scorpios are all the things that you hate most, and what makes it worse is that you can see what they're doing it for. They are secretive where you are frank, underhand where you are honest, and manipulative where you are generous. What they are trying to do is stay in control of everything. To them, it is important that the result of every action is known; if it is not, a situation leading to possible loss of control could result, leaving the Scorpio vulnerable to attack. They take great pains to assess the motivation of everybody they come into contact with, and are masters of interpersonal politics. If there is any plotting going on, then the Scorpio either knows about it, is doing it, or—very

Scorpio, this—suggested it. The amazing thing to you is that nobody can see this process going on; Scorpios take great care to keep their actions and feelings well hidden, and for the most part it works. It doesn't work with you, though; you can see into the situation without trying, and the devices of the Scorpio are quite visible to you. How angry this makes the Scorpio! How stupid he is made to feel, too, when you open a conversation by referring to some of his scheming, as in 'What are you doing hiding under the desk with a tape recorder, Scorpio?'

The fact that you seem not to care for your own safety, and are absurdly honest in your speech, makes him cringe in embarrassment; but the fact that you seem not only to get away with it but to benefit from it makes him grind his teeth with rage.

He sees you as a holy fool, protected by angels from the consequences of your naïvety. You see him as raging at his own insecurity, somebody who would be a lot better off if he could have the confidence to trust other people with himself. It's not really a good basis for a relationship.

For you to be good friends is unlikely. When you do have conversations, you will be aware of how much the Scorpio is trying to take off you, and how little he is willing to give in return. You would welcome his views on things, even if they were different to yours, but you know that he isn't going to let you know what he really thinks, and that annoys you. When you lose your temper, of course, he just smiles; other people's emotional outbursts are like food to him, because it puts him firmly in control of the situation.

A much likelier reason for you to be together is sexual attraction. Your ruling planets have much to do with it: Scorpio's Mars is a power for containment from outside, and your Jupiter is an irresistible expansion from within. Both of you enjoy the way the pressure rises when you are together. Scorpio is actually stronger than you are sexually, Sagittarius, but it won't be exhaustion that will make you decide you've had enough—his obsessive and possessive emotional energies will get to you first.

You don't like each other's methods enough to be reasonable business partners. As marriage partners, you would have to accept that the Scorpio will want to contain your energy, and that you would be unable to roam lest his awesome jealousy erupt. You would, of course, attempt to influence him for the better (as you would see it), but he will find it difficult to be as open or as flexible about things as you are. Present him with a variety of things and he simply tries to control all of them at the same time—he just can't let go. Eventually you would just get up and leave for good.

Sagittarius-Sagittarius
As with all the pairings between identical signs, this one has plenty to recommend it, and a few drawbacks as well. At least you are both Mutable signs, which means that you are both interested in examining a different point of view; if you were both dogmatic and unwilling to change your views at all, you would be in trouble from the start. You are both outgoing signs, too, which again brings benefits, because you are both willing to contribute to the situation; if you were both collecting signs, you would sit there each waiting for the other person to put something into the relationship.

So much for the good side of things. The trouble with this relationship is that you are both right. You both know all that there is to know about everything, and you both know it. You are therefore both right all the time; the trouble is that you are likely to be different. It is a difficult thing for a Sagittarian to understand that truth is essentially a personal concept, and that what seems true to one person may not be acceptable, or even credible, to another. If the other person is a Sagittarian like yourself you are doubly confused. You had thought that somebody like yourself would be able to see things the right way (i.e. your way), but it turns out not to be like that. You are also bothered because they are just as persuasive as you are, and their arguments are as clear and convincing as your own: it is all most unsettling.

Not that you spend much of your time deep in philosophical discussion, even though it does interest you greatly; you have other things to show each other. One of the great things about being a Sagittarius is your capacity to be inspired and excited by somebody else's interest, especially if it is new to you, and if they can communicate their own enthusiasm for it. Other signs retreat into themselves when faced with something unfamiliar, but you welcome it cheerfully. Obviously, another Sagittarian will have much to show you, and indeed much that he wants to show you; you welcome all of it. When you have a shared interest, you go off and do it together, but you don't get under each other's feet and you are not dependent on each other: these are the qualities you expect to find in others (because you have them in yourself) and you are delighted to find them in another Sagittarian.

A friendship between you may well be episodic in nature. Both of you have other things to do, and will go off and do them; when you both have time, perhaps you will see each other again, and talk about what you have been doing. Your friendship doesn't need to be regular to be enjoyable; it isn't formed from emotional dependency, but from a shared love of action and excitement. Something to look out for in a Sagittarian friendship is a tendency to talk about what you are hoping to do, rather than what you have already done; Sagittarian thought looks ever forward and upwards, and the future is more exciting to you than the past.

As lovers you will be evenly matched in terms of energy and inclinations, of course. You will be able to indulge in as much horseplay (don't ever forget the animal that forms your bottom half) as you want, and you gain much enjoyment from the knowledge that for both of you it is the spirit of the moment that counts. Love may well be for ever, but for you it must be right now as well.

As business partners you are hopeless: you both want to do the interesting bits, and neither of you can be bothered to stay up late doing the accounts. The same goes for a marriage: you are going to have to make sure that somebody does the household chores sometime. Not that either of you are great home-builders; as long as you have books to read, maps to plan your next journey together, and somewhere to sleep, you're quite happy.

Sagittarius-Capricorn

This is the most difficult of all the Sun-sign relationships for you to handle. It isn't that the Capricorn has any real trouble dealing with you, though he could think of other people he would rather be friends with, but that your planet, Jupiter, has a particular dislike for the sign of Capricorn. Capricorn is one of Saturn's two signs, of course, and Jupiter has never been too keen on Saturn; one planet tries to break out of all restraints, and the other tries to form closed frameworks. Read pages 23 and 24 again to remind yourself of what we are dealing with here.

You dislike Capricorn quite strongly. He seems on the one hand to have all the qualities you are trying to gain for yourself, which makes you envious, but he also seems to deserve them less, which offends your high principles.

If you remember the sequence of the zodiac signs you will get a better idea of what I mean. Sagittarius, as you know, is proud of his knowledge and perception. What he wants to do is to distribute this knowledge for the benefit of everybody, and to gain recognition and reputation as his reward. Capricorn, the next sign on, represents that reputation and recognition. Capricorn is what everybody sees as a man of reputation: the head of the company, the managing director, the big landowner, the plutocrat. You will notice at once that all these definitions contain images of money. That's what makes you mad: why is it, you ask, that the only reputation that seems to have any weight attached to it is a financial one? Why can't you be recognized for your ideas, in a Sagittarian way? The answer to that is that Capricorn is an Earth sign, and weight is of course a physical property, so therefore connected to physical matter, and hence to the element of Earth. Anything which has weight and importance on this planet is of the Earth; how do you think the planet got its name? (No, I'm not joking!)

Anyway, at the end of it all, the Capricorn has the money, the power, and the reputation, and you don't. You could live with this if it weren't for the fact that he hasn't got a fraction of your knowledge. Nor has he your warmth, your compassion, your imagination, your willingness to help, your spiritual depth, the nobility of your soul, or any of your optimism. In fact, he strikes you as a thoroughly uninspiring individual, and yet he has all the rewards this life can offer. Few things make you really angry, but this does.

He is quiet, methodical, and a really hard worker. He likes things ordered, and regular. He likes things to be in their places, and for there to be well-defined links between these places. He fits brilliantly into any corporate structure, and rises through it by regular hard work, and identification with the corporation. In other words, he's a company man.

You couldn't imagine anything worse, could you? No imagination, no freedom, no impulsiveness. No far horizons, no knowledge, no vision.

He sees you in an equally unflattering light. You have no organization, no structure. You won't wait for anything; you have no sense of time. You have no reserve, no tact; you also pay no respect to your superiors. Worst of all, you give things away—knowledge, warmth, companionship. Why can't you see that if you have things that other people want, then you should sell them, not give them away? No wonder you have no money.

From this you will understand that a friendship between you will be almost impossible. If you tell a Capricorn anything, he will use it to advance his own reputation, not yours. In addition, if you refuse to recognize him as the successful person he is, he will end the friendship—to the Capricorn if there is no reward then it is not worthwhile.

As lovers, your motives are somewhat different. Physically, everything will be fine—Capricorns have a goat for their animal, so you know what to expect—but deep down, you make love for fun, and they make love as part of a career plan.

As business partners, you can do very well, if you are prepared to take it seriously. Capricorns are wonderful businessmen anyway, but they lack your entrepreneurial spirit. If you provide that, and direct your energies firmly to the job in hand, then Capricorn will see to it that you both become very wealthy.

Marriage? Possibly—but it isn't a love match, it's an arrangement, a private deal. You give all your warmth and knowledge to them, and they give all their practical management skills to you. The result is that your ideas and personality get converted into money, and they have the pleasure of your company and talent as an exclusive right, which appeals to the snob in them. Not a bad arrangement—but short on romance, so be warned.

Sagittarius-Aquarius

It is difficult to comprehend how two signs, ruled by the same planet, could be so different in their attitude towards you, but there it is: Capricorn and Aquarius are both Saturn's signs, but where the Capricorn pairing is almost impossibly hard, this one is delightfully easy. It is similar, in many ways, to the Libra partnership.

Aquarius is a bit of a paradox, but since both sides of it appeal to you, there are no problems. On the one hand, an Aquarian loves company, and is always involved with some social group or other, but on the other hand, he feels that he is different from everybody else, and is attracted to anything unusual, or which makes him stand apart from the crowd. All of this is fine by you—you like a varied social life too, and anything which is different you find interesting.

Aquarius is an Air sign, as Libra and Gemini are, and as in those relationships, this is one where you seem to have a lot to talk about. Aquarians don't have your depth of insight, but they have a refreshingly wide range of interests, and they get quite passionate when talking about issues which arouse their concern. This means that you can have a good argument with an Aquarian, pulling at the subject between you like two dogs with a stick, and both enjoying the affair enormously. Only the two of you will realize that you *like* this process; other signs will be horrified at what they see as bitter feuding, though Gemini will appreciate what you are up to, and probably join in for the hell of it. The difference between Aquarius and Gemini, as far as you're concerned, is that you really disagree quite fundamentally with what the Gemini is doing, whereas most of the time you are in agreement with the Aquarian's principles, and that makes your arguments much more playful affairs.

Principles are funny things; to have them, you have to be able to look outside yourself, and think of the wider implications of things. Both you and Aquarius have high principles, and you appreciate this in each other. In the Aquarius, it often shows as a particular political persuasion, or a devotion to humanitarian causes. Another thing you might notice is how determinedly egalitarian they are. In an Aquarian's world, everybody is equal, and all hierarchies or master-and-servant relationships are seen as a bad thing. This isn't so far removed from your own view that respect is given rather than demanded, and that everybody should be free to do what they please.

You see them as talkative and sociable people, who believe in good causes and are prepared to argue their case. They see you as refreshingly enthusiastic friends, honest and loyal, not afraid to speak your mind, and with the right sort of ideas about most things.

A friendship between you is a very easy thing to produce. You find a great deal of comfort in knowing somebody who is likely to understand what you are trying to say, but is not necessarily going to agree with your opinion in every case. It is also good, in your eyes at least, to have a friend who doesn't want to be too closely tied to you emotionally; Aquarians are quite cool in that respect, and they understand your need for freedom very well, since it is similar to their own need to be independent.

As lovers, you are very well suited. They have plenty of physical stamina, and they like playing, but they don't need deep emotional commitment. That's just how you like it.

Business partners? Maybe, if you can find something which maintains your interest and doesn't offend your principles. You're good as a team, but are you really businessmen at heart? Marriage would be a much better bet—a lively, open partnership, looking forwards to a better future. You might find that it lacked a sense of traditional family values, but you could supply that.

Sagittarius-Pisces

A very interesting partnership, as indeed all relationships involving Pisces are. It is a sign containing every possibility, but often it doesn't know which one to choose. Nothing about the Piscean is clear-cut; when you try to pin them down, they run through your fingers. It's what you would expect from Mutable Water, if you think about it.

The zodiac comes up with some strange combinations, and this is one of the strangest. Although you are of different elements, representing different directions (they are incoming, you are outgoing) in different universes (they are imaginary, you are real), you are ruled to the same planet—Jupiter. All that expansion and growth, all that energy for increase, is *inverted* in the Piscean. Where you radiate energy and enthusiasm outwards, exploring distant lands, and gathering experience and knowledge, they are expanding inwards, discovering new and more fantastic realms of experience and sensation inside themselves, painting ever more complex patterns on the *insides* of their heads. Fascinating idea, isn't it?

They are sensitive and imaginative like nobody else in the zodiac. These people can think in terms of colour and music, drama and poetry, and sometimes all of them at once, in a way which you find compelling. They can be anything they want; they take their cues from the situation they find themselves in, and somehow manage to be all things to all men. The whole business fascinates you; your curiosity wants to know what the real nature of the Piscean is, under all the disguises.

There isn't one. They really are who they say they are at the time. There is a fundamental difference between you, which, although it sounds far removed from daily life, actually underlies everything you do together, and it is this:

You think that once you know something, it is an unalterable fact for ever. The truth never changes, in your view. The Piscean knows that today's answer may not be quite so true tomorrow. In his view, truth is defined by the person to whom it seems true, and that person is constantly changing.

So the Piscean is as keen to know things as you are, but he enjoys the way that what he knows changes as time goes by. You can sense this somehow, and you are very curious to experience it for yourself.

You see them as fascinating creatures, so sensitive that the slightest stimulus will set their imaginations off into flights of creative fantasy. You can't quite see all this as being useful, though, and you have the sneaky feeling that a lot of your own knowledge may be similarly viewed by others.

They see you as great sources of creative energy, enough for you to wear your ideas on the outside, which they find very impressive. They see your clarity of thought as particularly desirable, because in your case you do appear to have compromised your imagination to obtain your logical approach. Because you are so much more confident and expressive than they are, they see you as an admirable blend of creative imagination and worldly success. This isn't quite right, as you will no doubt tell them, because you are honest that way, but you must admit that it's very flattering of them to see you in those terms.

Friendship between you is formed out of mutual curiosity and admiration rather than what you have in common. You have conversations like magicians practising their art on each other; you give them ideas to see what the Piscean does with them, and they give you impressions of things from which you try to guess the original stimulus. Like Art, these encounters work on more than one level at once; you find it exacting but satisfying, and although you think you know what you get out of it, you probably couldn't explain it to anybody else.

Should you become lovers, you will find yourselves communicating on two more levels simultaneously—the animal and the spiritual. You will have to be a little less robust in your approach than is usual for you, but when it all works you will discover dimensions of yourself you never knew you had.

As business partners you would only do really well if you were in a media-related business. You are both too good with ideas and not good enough with routines, finances and organization to feel at home in a traditional business structure.

If you married, you would be happy enough, but unless one of you has a practical streak somewhere, you would need all sorts of help to manage your finances and do things like fix the plumbing. Not that you'd care: in this marriage, material things are definitely a low priority.

Part 3

Your Life

5. The Year within Each Day

You have probably wondered, in odd moments, why there are more than twelve varieties of people. You know more than twelve people who look completely different. You also know more than one person with the same Sun sign as yourself who doesn't look anything like you. You also know two people who look quite like each other, but who are not related, and do not have birthdays near each other, so can't be of the same Sun sign. You will have come to the conclusion that Sun signs and astrology don't work too well, because anyone can see that there are more than twelve sorts of people.

You will also have wondered, as you finished reading a newspaper or magazine horoscope, how those few sentences manage to apply to a twelfth of the nation, and why it is that they are sometimes very close to your true circumstances, and yet at other times miles off. You will have come to the conclusion that astrology isn't all that it might be, but some of it is, and that you like it enough to buy magazines for the horoscopes, and little books like this one.

It might be that there is some other astrological factor, or factors, which account for all the different faces that people have, the similarities between people of different Sun signs, and the apparent inconsistencies in magazine horoscopes. There are, indeed, lots of other astrological factors we could consider, but one in particular will answer most of the inconsistencies we have noticed so far.

It is the Ascendant, or rising sign. Once you know your Ascendant, you will see how you get your appearance, your way of working, your tastes, your preferences and dislikes, and your state of health (or not, as the case may be). It is perhaps of more use to you to consider yourself as belonging to your Ascendant sign, than your Sun sign. You have been reading the wrong newspaper horoscopes for years; you are not who you thought you were!

You are about to protest that you know when your birthday is. I'm sure you do. This system is not primarily linked to your birthday, though. It is a smaller cogwheel in the clockwork of the heavens, and we must come down one level from where we have been standing to see its movements. Since astrology is basically the large patterns of the sky made small in an individual, there are a number of 'step-down' processes where the celestial machinery adjusts itself to the smaller scale of mankind; this is one of them.

Here's the theory:

Your birthday pinpoints a particular time during the year. The Sun appears to move round the strip of sky known as the zodiac during the course of the year. In reality, of course, our planet, Earth, moves round the Sun once a year, but the great friendly feature of astrology is that it always looks at things from our point of view; so, we think we stand still, and the Sun appears to move through the zodiac. On a particular day of importance, such as your birthday, you can see which of the zodiac signs the Sun is in, pinpoint how far it has gone in its annual trip round the sky, and then say 'This day is important to me, because it is my birthday; therefore this part of the sky is important to me because the Sun is there on my special day. What are the qualities of that part of the Sun's journey through the zodiac, and what are they when related to me?' The answer is what you usually get in a horoscope book describing your Sun sign.

Fine. Now let's go down one level, and get some more detail. The Earth rotates on its own axis every day. This means that, from our point of view, we stand still and the sky goes round us once a day. Perhaps you hadn't thought of it before, but that's how the Sun appears to move up and across the sky from sunrise to sunset. It's actually us who are moving, but we see it the other way round. During any day, then, your birthday included, the whole of the sky goes past you at some time or another; but at a particular moment of importance, such as the time that you were born, you can see where the Sun is, see which way up the sky is, and say, 'This moment is important to me, because I was born at this time; therefore the layout of the sky has the same qualities as I do. What are the qualities of the sky at this time of day, and what are they when related to me?'

You can see how you are asking the same questions one level lower down. The problem is that you don't know which bit of the sky is significant. Which bit do you look at? All you can see? All that you can't (it's spherical from your point of view, and has no joins; half of it is below the horizon, remember)?

How about directly overhead? A very good try; the point in the zodiac you would arrive at is indeed significant, and is used a lot by astrologers, but there is another one which is more useful still. The eastern horizon is the point used most. Why? Because it fulfils more functions than any other point. It gives a starting point which is easily measurable, and is even visible (remember, all astrology started from observations made before mathematics or telescopes). It is also the contact point between the sky and the earth, from our point of view, and thus symbolizes the relationship between the sky and mankind on the earth. Finally, it links the smaller cycle of the day to the larger one of the year, because the Sun starts its journey on the eastern horizon each day as it rises; and, if we are concerned with a special moment, such as the time of your birth, then the start of the day, or the place that it started, at any rate, is analogous to the start of your life. Remember that you live the qualities of the moment you were born for all of your life; you are that moment made animate.

The point in the zodiac, then, which was crossing the eastern horizon at the time you were born, is called the Ascendant. If this happened to be somewhere in the middle of Gemini, then you have a Gemini Ascendant, or Gemini rising, whichever phrase you prefer. You will see that this has nothing to do with the time

| STAR TIME (HOURS) | 0 | 1 | 2 | 3 | 4 | 5 | 6 | 7 | 8 | 9 | 10 | 11 | 12 | 13 | 14 | 15 | 16 | 17 | 18 | 19 | 20 | 21 | 22 | 23 | 0 |

GLASGOW: LEO · VIRGO · LIBRA · SCORPIO · SAGITTARIUS · CAPRICORN · AQUARIUS · PISCES · ARIES · TAURUS · GEMINI · CANCER · LEO

MAN-CHESTER: LEO · VIRGO · LIBRA · SCORPIO · SAGITTARIUS · CAPRICORN · AQUARIUS · PISCES · ARIES · TAURUS · GEMINI · CANCER

LONDON: CANCER · LEO · VIRGO · LIBRA · SCORPIO · SAGITTARIUS · CAPRICORN · AQUARIUS · PISCES · ARIES · TAURUS · GEMINI · CANCER

Different signs are on the horizon at different times according to where you live, as you can see. This is because of the difference in latitude. If you live in between the places given, you can make a guess from the values here. To compensate for longitude, subtract twelve minutes from your birthtime if you live in Glasgow, Liverpool or Cardiff; ten minutes for Edinburgh or Manchester, and six minutes for Leeds, Tyneside, or the West Midlands. *Add* four minutes for Norwich.

of year that you were born, only with the time of day.

Have a look at the diagram opposite, which should help explain things. If two people are born on the same day, but at different times, then the Ascendant will be different, and the Sun and all the other planets will be occupying different parts of the sky. It makes sense to assume, then, that they will be different in a number of ways. Their lives will be different, and they will look different. What they will have in common is the force of the Sun in the same sign, but it will show itself in different ways because of the difference in time and position in the sky.

How do you know which sign was rising over the eastern horizon when you were born? You will have to work it out. In the past, the calculation of the Ascendant has been the subject of much fuss and secrecy, which astrologers exploit to the full, claiming that only they can calculate such things. It does take some doing, it is true, but with a few short cuts and a calculator it need only take five minutes.

Here is the simplest routine ever devised for you to calculate your own Ascendant, provided that you know your time of birth. Pencil your answers alongside the stages as you go, so you know where you are.

1. Count forwards from 22 November to your birthday: 22 November is 1, 23 November is 2, and so on.
   Total days: ....23........................

2. Add 61 to this. New total is: ....84.................

3. Divide by 365, and then

4. Multiply by 24. Answer is now: ..5.5....................
   (Your answer by now is between 0 and 24. If it isn't, you have made a mistake somewhere. Go back and try again.)

5. Add your time of birth, in 24-hour clock time. If you were born at 3 p.m., that means 15. If you were born in Summer Time, take one hour off. If there are some spare minutes, your calculator would probably like them in decimals, so it's 0.1 of an hour for each six minutes. 5.36 p.m. is 17.6, for example. Try to be as close as you can. New total is: ..23.5.....

6. If your total exceeds 24, subtract 24. Your answer must now be between 0 and 24. Answer is: . .23.5. . . . .

7. You have now got the time of your birth not in clock time, but in sidereal, or star, time, which is what astrologers work in. Page 72 has a strip diagram with the signs of the zodiac arranged against a strip with the values 0 to 24, which are hours in star time. Look against the time you have just calculated, and you will see which sign was rising at the time you were born. For example, if your calculated answer is 10.456, then your Ascendant is about the 16th degree of Scorpio

What Does the Ascendant Do?

Broadly speaking, the Ascendant does two things. Firstly, it gives you a handle on the sky, so that you know which way up it was at the time you entered the game, so to speak; this has great significance later on in the book, when we look at the way you handle large areas of activity in your life such as your career, finances, and ambitions. Secondly, it describes your body. If you see your Sun sign as your mentality and way of thinking, then your Ascendant sign is your body and your way of doing things. Think of your Sun sign as the true you, but the Ascendant as the vehicle you have to drive through life. It is the only one you have, so you can only do with it the things of which it is capable, and there may be times when you would like to do things in a different way, but it 'just isn't you'. What happens over your life is that your Sun sign energies become specifically adapted to express themselves to their best via your Ascendant sign, and you become an amalgam of the two. If you didn't, you would soon become very ill. As an Sagittarius with, say, an Aquarian Ascendant, you do things from a Sagittarius motivation, but in an Aquarian way, using an Aquarian set of talents and abilities, and an Aquarian body. The next few sections of the book explain what this means for each of the Sun/Ascendant combinations.

Some note ought to be made of the correspondence between the Ascendant and the actual condition of the body. Since the

Ascendant sign represents your physical frame rather than the personality inside it, then the appearance and well-being of that frame is also determined by the Ascendant sign. In other words, if you have a Libra Ascendant, then you should look like a Libran, and you should be subject to illnesses in the parts of the body with a special affinity to that sign.

The Astrology of Illness

This is worth a book in itself, but it is quite important to say that the astrological view of illness is that the correlation between the individual and the larger universe is maintained. In other words, if you continue over a long period of time with a way of behaviour that denies the proper and necessary expression of your planetary energies, then the organ of your body which normally handles that kind of activity for your body systems will start to show the stresses to you. A simple example: Gemini looks after the lungs, which circulate air, and from which oxygen is taken all over the body. Gemini people need to circulate among a lot of people, talking and exchanging information. They act as the lungs of society, taking news and information everywhere. They need to do this to express their planetary energies, and society needs them to do this or it is not refreshed, and does not communicate. You need your lungs to do this, too. Lungs within people, Geminis within society: same job, different levels. If you keep a Gemini, or he keeps himself, through circumstance or ignorance, in a situation where he cannot talk or circulate, or where he feels that his normal status is denied, then he is likely to develop lung trouble. This need not be anything to do with a dusty atmosphere, or whether he smokes, although obviously neither of those will help; they are external irritants, and this is an internal problem caused by imbalance in the expression of the energies built into him since birth. In the sections which follow, all the observations on health are to do with how the body shows you that certain behaviour is unbalancing you and causing unnecessary stress; problems from these causes are alleviated by listening to yourself and changing your behaviour.

Your Ascendant

Aries Ascendant

If you have Aries rising, you are an uncommon individual, because Aries only rises for about fifty minutes out of the twenty-four hour day. You must have been born in the middle of the afternoon, or else you have got your sums wrong somewhere.

What you are trying to do with yourself is project a Sagittarian personality through an Arian vehicle. You will always be trying to do things faster than anybody else, and this can lead to hastiness and a certain degree of accident-proneness. What you see as the correct way to do things involves immediate action by the most direct method, to secure instant, and measurable, results. You feel that unless you are directly and personally responsible for doing things, then they cannot be done, not only because you believe that only you can do them properly, but because you get no satisfaction from letting anybody else do anything. Personal experience of everything is the only way you learn; reading about it, or watching it, does nothing for you.

You are likely to have headaches as a recurring problem if you push yourself too hard, and you should watch your blood pressure too. Mars, ruling Aries, is a strong and forceful planet, and it is bound to get you a little over-stressed at times. You are also likely to have problems digesting things properly. Astrologically, all illnesses apply to your external condition as well as your internal condition, so think carefully; when your head aches you are banging it too hard against a problem which cannot be overcome that way, and when you are not digesting properly, you have not understood the implications of what you have taken on. In both cases, allow time to think and consider.

Taurus Ascendant

You were born in the middle of the afternoon if you have Taurus rising. Taureans are generally fond of food—did you arrive in time for tea, or were you a little early? You should have all the Taurean physical characteristics: quite thick-set, big around the neck and shoulders sometimes, and with large hands. You should have a broad mouth, and large eyes, which are very attractive. You should also have a good voice—not only as a singing voice, but one which is pleasant to listen to in conversation too.

The Taurean method for getting things done is to look forward to, and then enjoy, the material reward for one's efforts. It is part of Taurean thinking that if you can't touch it, buy it, own it or eat it, it isn't real and it isn't worth much. You will also be concerned to keep what is yours, not to waste your energies on what won't gain you anything or increase your possessions, and not to attempt anything which you don't think you have more than a chance of achieving.

Taureans do have taste; not only taste for food, which they love, but artistic taste, which they develop as a means of distinguishing things of value which they would then like to acquire and gain pleasure from owning. Unlike the Capricorn way of doing things, which values quality because it is valued by others, Taureans enjoy their possessions for themselves. The drawback to the Taurean approach is the lack of enterprise, and the unwillingness to try things just for the fun of it.

Taurean Ascendant people have throat and glandular problems, and all problems associated with being overweight. They can also have back and kidney problems caused as a result of an unwillingness to let things go in their external life. A lighter touch is needed in the approach to problems of possession; shedding unwanted or outworn things in a desirable process.

Gemini Ascendant

If you have a Gemini Ascendant you were born somewhere around sunset. You should have expressive hands and a wide range of gestures which you use as you speak (ask your friends!) and you are perhaps a little taller than average, or than other members of your family. Gemini Ascendant people also have dark hair, if there is any possibility of it in their parents' colouring, and quick, penetrating eyes which flash with amusement and mischief; Gemini Ascendant women have very fine eyes indeed.

The Gemini approach to things, which you find yourself using, is one in which the idea of a thing is seen as being the most useful, and in which no time must be lost in telling it to other people so that they can contribute their own ideas and responses to the discussion. The performance of the deed is of no real importance in the Gemini view; somebody else can do that. Ideas and their development are what you like to spend time on, and finding more people to talk to, whose ideas can be matched to your own, seems to you to offer the most satisfaction.

There are two snags to the Gemini approach. The first is that there is a surface quality to it all, in which the rough outline suffices, but no time is spent in development or long-term experience. It may seem insignificant, but there is some value in seeing a project through to the end. The second snag is similar, but is concerned with time. The Gemini approach is immediate, in that it is concerned with the present or the near future. It is difficult for a Gemini Ascendant person to see farther than a few months into the future, if that; it is even more difficult for him to extend his view sideways in time to see the impact of his actions on a wider scene. Both of these things he will dismiss as unimportant.

Gemini Ascendant people suffer from chest and lung maladies, especially when they cannot communicate what they want to or need to, or when they cannot circulate socially in the way that they would like. They also have problems eliminating wastes from their bodies, through not realizing the importance of ending things as well as beginning them. In both cases, thinking and planning on a broader scale than usual, and examination of the past to help make better use of the future, is beneficial.

Cancer Ascendant
You were born in the early evening if you have your Ascendant in Cancer and your Sun in Sagittarius. The Cancerian frame, through which you project your energies, may mean that you appear rounder and less long-limbed than other Sagittarians. Your energies are in no way diminished; in fact, you are likely to be even more determined to get things right. Your face could be

almost cherubic, and you could have small features in a pale complexion with grey eyes and brown hair. The key to the Cancer frame is that it is paler than usual, less well defined than usual, and has no strong colouring. Strong noses and red hair do not come from a Cancerian Ascendant.

The Cancerian approach to things is highly personal. All general criticisms are taken personally, and all problems in any procedure for which they have responsibility is seen as a personal failing. You will be concerned to use your energies for the safe and secure establishment of things from the foundations up, so that you know that whatever you have been involved in has been done properly, and is unlikely to let you down in any way; you are concerned for your own safety and reputation. The other side of this approach is that you can be a little too concerned to make sure everything is done personally, and be unwilling to entrust things to other people. Not only does this overwork you, it seems obsessive and uncooperative to others.

The Cancer Ascendant person has health problems with the maintenance of the flow of fluids in his body, and a tendency to stomach ulcers caused by worry. Cancer Ascendant women should pay special attention to their breasts, since the affinity between the sign, the Moon as ruler of all things feminine, and that particular body system means that major imbalances in the life are likely to show there first. There could also be some problems with the liver and the circulation of the legs; the answer is to think that, metaphorically, you do not have to support everybody you know: they can use their own legs to stand on, and you do not have to feed them either.

Leo Ascendant

You were born late in the evening if you have Leo as an Ascendant. Leo, as the determinant of the physical characteristics, makes itself known by the lion of the sign—you can always spot the deep chest, proud and slightly pompous way of walking, and, more often than not, the hair arranged in some sort of a mane, either full or taken back off the face, and golden if possible. Leo Ascendant people have strong voices and a definite presence to them. A Leo Ascendant will bring to the fore any hereditary tendency to golden colouring, so reddish or golden hair, or a rosy complexion may be in evidence, as will a heavy build in the upper half of the body.

The Leonine way of doing things is to put yourself in the centre and work from the centre outwards, making sure that everybody knows where the commands are coming from. It is quite a tiring way of working; you need to put a lot of energy into it, because you are acting as the driving force for everybody else. Preferred situations for this technique are those where you already know, more or less, what's going to happen; this way you are unlikely to be thrown off balance by unexpected developments. The grand gesture belongs to the Leo method; it works best if all processes are converted into theatrical scenes, with roles acted rather than lived. Over-reaction, over-dramatization, and over-indulgence are common, but the approach is in essence kind-hearted and well-meant. Children enjoy being with Leo Ascendant people, and they enjoy having children around them. The flaws in the approach are only that little gets done in difficult circumstances where applause and appreciation are scarce commodities, and that little is attempted that is really new and innovatory.

The health problems of the Leo Ascendant person come from the heart, and also from the joints, which suffer from mobility problems. These both come from a lifetime of being at the centre of things and working for everybody's good, and from being too stiff and unwilling to try any change in position. The remedy, of course, is to be more flexible, and to allow your friends to repay the favours they owe you.

Virgo Ascendant

A birth around midnight puts Virgo on the Ascendant. Physically, this should make you slim and rather long, especially in the body; even if you have broad shoulders you will still have a long waist. There is a neatness to the features, but nothing notable; hair is brown, but again nothing notable. The nose and chin are often well-defined, and the forehead is often both tall and broad;

the voice can be a little shrill and lacks penetration.

The Virgoan Ascendant person does not have an approach to life; he has a *system*. He analyses everything and pays a lot of attention to the way in which he works. It is important to the person with Virgo rising not only to be effective, but to be efficient; you can always interest them in a new or better technique. They watch themselves work, as if from a distance, all the while wondering if they can do it better. They never mind repetition; in fact they quite enjoy it, because as they get more proficient they feel better about things. To you, being able to do things is everything, and unless you are given a practical outlet for your energies, you are completely ineffective. There is a willingness to help others, to be of service through being able to offer a superior technique, inherent in the Virgo way of doing things, which prevents Virgo rising people from being seen as cold and unfriendly. They appreciate their help being appreciated. The problems in the Virgo attitude are a tendency to go into things in more detail than is necessary, and to be too much concerned with the 'proper' way to do things.

People with a Virgo Ascendant are susceptible to intestinal problems, and also circulatory problems, and maybe poor sight. All of these are ways in which the body registers the stresses of being too concerned with digesting the minutiae of things which are meant to be passed through anyway, and by not getting enough social contact. The remedy is to lift your head from your workbench sometimes, admit that the act is sometimes more important than the manner of its performance, and not to take things too seriously.

Libra Ascendant

You were born in the small hours of the morning if you have Libra rising; it will give you a pleasant and approachable manner which will do a great deal to hide your anxieties and prevent people thinking anything but the best of you. You should be tallish, and graceful, as all Libra Ascendant people tend to be; they have a clear complexion, and blue eyes if possible, set in an oval face with finely formed features.

The Libra Ascendant person has to go through life at a fairly relaxed pace. The sign that controls his body won't let him feel rushed or anxious; if that sort of thing looks likely, then he will slow down a little until the panic's over. There is a need to see yourself reflected in the eyes of others, and so you will form a large circle of friends. You define your own opinion of yourself through their responses to you, rather than being sure what you want, and not caring what they think.

The drawback to the Libran approach is that unless you have approval from others, you are unlikely to do anything on your own initiative, or at least you find it hard to decide on a course of action. You always want to do things in the way which will cause the least bother to anyone, and to produce an acceptable overall result; sometimes this isn't definite enough, and you need to know what you do want as well as what you don't.

The Libran Ascendant makes the body susceptible to all ailments of the kidneys and of the skin; there may also be trouble in the feet. The kidney ailments are from trying to take all the problems out of life as you go along. Sometimes it's better simply to attack a few of the obstacles and knock them flat in pure rage—and in doing so you will develop adrenaline from the adrenal glands, on top of the kidneys!

Scorpio Ascendant
You were born in time for breakfast if you have a Scorpio Ascendant. It should give you a dark and powerful look, with a solid build, though not necessarily over-muscled, Scorpio Ascendant people tend to have a very penetrating and level way of looking at others, which is often disconcerting. Any possible darkness in the colouring is usually displayed, with dark complexions and dark hair, often thick and curly, never fine.

The Scorpio Ascendant person usually does things in a controlled manner. He is not given to explosive releases of energy unless they are absolutely necessary; even then, not often. He knows, or feels (a better word, since the Scorpionic mind makes decisions as a result of knowledge gained by feeling rather than thinking), that he has plenty of energy to spare, but uses it in small and effective doses, each one suited to the requirements of the task at hand. It does not seem useful to him to put in more effort than is strictly necessary for any one activity; that extra energy could be used somewhere else. The idea that overdoing things for their own sake is sometimes fun because of the sheer exhilaration of the release of energy does not strike a responsive chord in the Scorpio body, nor even much understanding. There is, however, understanding and perception of a situation which exists at more than one level. If anything is complicated, involving many activities and many people, with much interaction and many side issues which must be considered, then the Scorpio Ascendant person sees it all and understands all of it, in its minutest detail. They feel, and understand, the responses from all of their surroundings at once, but do not necessarily feel involved with them unless they choose to make a move. When they do move, they will have the intention of transforming things, making them different to conform to their ideas of how things need to be arranged.

Scorpio Ascendant people are unable simply to possess and look after anything; they must change it and direct it their way, and this can be a disadvantage.

Scorpio illnesses are usually to do with the genital and excretory systems; problems here relate to a lifestyle in which things are thrown away when used, or sometimes rejected when there is still use in them. It may be that there is too much stress on being the founder of the new, and on organizing others; this will bring head pains, and illnesses of that order. The solution is to take on the existing situation as it is, and look after it without changing any of it.

Sagittarius Ascendant

It would have been sunrise when you were born for you to have a Sagittarius Ascendant as well as a Sagittarius Sun. If you have, you should be taller than average, with a sort of sporty, leggy look to you; you should have a long face with pronounced temples (you may be balding there if you are a male), a well-coloured complexion, clear eyes, and brown hair. A Grecian nose is sometimes a feature of this physique.

The Sagittarian Ascendant gives a way of working that is based on mobility and change. This particular frame can't keep still and is much more comfortable walking than standing, more comfortable lounging or leaning than sitting formally. You tend to be in a bit of a hurry; travelling takes up a lot of your time, because you enjoy it so. It is probably true to say that you enjoy the process of driving more than whatever it is that you have to do when you get there. You probably think a lot of your car, and you are likely to have one which is more than just a machine for transport—you see it as an extension, a representation even, of yourself. People will notice how outgoing and friendly you seem to be, but they will need to know you for some time before they realize that you enjoy meeting people more than almost anything else, and you dislike being with the same companions all the time. There is a constant restlessness in you; you will feel that being static is somehow unnatural, and it worries you. You are an optimist, but can also be an opportunist, in that you see no reason to stay doing one thing for a moment longer than it interests you. The inability to stay and develop a situation or give long-term commitment to anything is the biggest failing of this sign's influence.

A person with Sagittarius rising can expect to have problems with his hips and thighs, and possibly in his arterial system; this is to do with trying to leap too far at once, in all senses. You may also have liver and digestive problems, again caused by haste on a long-term scale. The remedy is to shorten your horizons and concentrate on things nearer home.

Capricorn Ascendant

It must have been mid-morning when you were born for you to have a Capricorn Ascendant. This sign often gives a small frame, quite compact and built to last a long time, the sort that doesn't need a lot of feeding and isn't big enough or heavy enough to break when it falls over. The face can be narrow and the features small; often the mouth points downwards at the corners, and this doesn't change even when the person smiles or laughs.

The Capricorn sees life as an ordered, dutiful struggle. There is a great deal of emphasis placed on projecting and maintaining appearances, both in the professional and the personal life; the idea of 'good reputation' is one which everybody with Capricorn rising, whatever their sun sign, recognizes at once. There is a sense of duty and commitment which the Sagittarian Ascendant simply cannot understand; here the feeling is that there are things which need doing, so you just have to set to and get them done. Capricorn Ascendant people see far forwards in time, anticipating their responsibilities for years to come, even if their Sun sign does not normally function this way; in such cases they apply themselves to one problem at a time, but can envisage a succession of such problems, one after another, going on for years.

The disadvantages of this outlook are to do with its static nature. There is often a sense of caution that borders on the paranoid, and while this is often well disguised in affluent middle-class middle age, it seems a little odd in the young. This tends to make for a critical assessment of all aspects of a new venture before embarking on it, and as a result a lot of the original impetus is lost. This makes the result less than was originally hoped in many cases, and so a cycle of disappointment and unadventurousness sets in, which is difficult to break. The Capricorn Ascendant person is often humourless, and can seem determined to remain so.

These people have trouble in their joints, and break bones from time to time, entirely as a result of being inflexible. On a small scale this can be from landing badly in an accident because the Capricorn Ascendant keeps up appearances to the very end, refusing to believe that an accident could be happening to him: on a large scale, a refusal to move with the times can lead to the collapse of an outmoded set of values when they are swept away by progress, and this breaking up of an old structure can also cripple. They can get lung troubles, too, as a result of not taking enough fresh air, or fresh ideas. The best treatment is to look after their families rather than their reputation, and to think about the difference between stability and stagnation.

Aquarius Ascendant

Having an Aquarius Ascendant means that you were born in the late morning. This will make you more sociable than you would otherwise have been, with a strong interest in verbal communication. An Aquarian Ascendant will also make for great success in your chosen career, whatever it is. No matter what the job is, being born around the middle of the day guarantees public prominence whether you want it or not.

There is a certain clarity, not to say transparency, about the Aquarian physique. It is usually tall, fair, and well shaped, almost never small or dark. There is nothing about the face which is particularly distinctive; no noticeable colouring, shape of nose, brows, or any other feature. It is an average sort of face, cleanly formed and clear.

The person with an Aquarian Ascendant wants to be independent. Not violently so, not the sort of independence that fights its way out of wherever it feels it's been put, just different from everybody else. Aquarius gives your body the ability to do things in ways perhaps not done before; you can discover new techniques and practices for yourself, and don't need to stay in the ways you were taught. There is a willingness to branch out, to try new things; not a Scorpionic wish to make things happen the way you want, but an amused curiosity which would just like to see if things are any better done a different way. There is no need for you to convince the world that your way is best: it only needs to suit you.

Of course, an Aquarian needs to measure his difference against others, and therefore you feel better when you have a few friends around you to bounce ideas off, as well as showing them how you're doing things in a slightly different way. You function best in groups, and feel physically at ease when you're not the only person in the room. You are not necessarily the leader of the group; just a group member. Group leaders put their energy into the group, and you draw strength and support from it, so you are unlikely to be the leader, though paradoxically all groups work better for having you in them.

A handicap arising from an Aquarian Ascendant is that you

are unlikely to really feel passionately involved with anything, and this may mean that unless you have support from your friends and colleagues you will be unable to muster the determination necessary to overcome really sizeable obstacles in your chosen career.

You are likely to suffer from diseases of the circulation and in your lower legs and ankles; these may reflect a life where too much time is spent trying to be independent, and not enough support is sought from others. You may also get stomach disorders and colds because you are not generating enough heat: get more involved in things and angrier about them!

Pisces Ascendant

You were born around noon if you have Pisces rising. Like Aries rising, Pisces is only possible as an Ascendant for about fifty minutes, so there aren't many of you around. A Piscean Ascendant will also make for great success in your chosen career, particularly if you are a late Sagittarian. No matter what the job is, being born around the middle of the day guarantees public prominence whether you want it or not. The same applies to early Sagittarians and Aquarius rising; the essential thing is to be born just a little *before* noon for this effect to be really marked. Pisces Ascendant people are on the small side, with a tendency to be a bit pale and fleshy. They are not very well coordinated and so walk rather clumsily, despite the fact that their feet are often large. They have large, expressive, but rather sleepy-looking eyes.

As a Sagittarian with Pisces rising, you will prefer to let things come to you than go out and look for them; you are the least assertive of all the Sagittarians. A Piscean Ascendant will help you really get the most out of your Sagittarian travelling, though. Not only will you enjoy visiting different places, but while you are there you will become part of them—something the ordinary tourist cannot hope to achieve. Pisces rising will also make you sensitive to other people's thoughts in a way that Sagittarians usually aren't. You will be able to see what other people feel, as well as knowing what's right as you usually do – an unusually perceptive combination.

The major problem with a Pisces Ascendant is this inability to be active rather than reactive; you would rather be reacting to outside influences than generating your own movements from within yourself.

A Piscean Ascendant gives problems with the feet and the lymphatic system; this has connections with the way you move in response to external pressures, and how you deal with things which invade your system from outside. You may also suffer from faint-heartedness—literally as well as metaphorically. The remedy is to be more definite and less influenced by opinions other than your own.

6. Three Crosses: Areas of Life that Affect Each Other

If you have already determined your Ascendant sign from page 74, and you have read 'The Meaning of the Zodiac' on page 11, you can apply that knowledge to every area of your life with revealing results. Instead of just looking at yourself, you can see how things like your career and your finances work from the unique point of view of your birth moment.

You will remember how the Ascendant defined which way up the sky was. Once you have it the right way up, then you can divide it into sectors for different areas of life, and see which zodiac signs occupy them. After that, you can interpret each sector of sky in the light of what you know about the zodiac sign which fell in it at the time that you were born.

Below there is a circular diagram of the sky, with the horizon splitting it across the middle. This is the way real horoscopes are usually drawn. In the outer circle, in the space indicated, write the name of your Ascendant sign, not your Sun sign (unless they are the same, of course. If you don't know your time of birth, and so can't work out an Ascendant, use your Sun sign.) Make it overlap sectors 12 and 1, so that the degree of your Ascendant within that sign is on the Eastern Horizon. Now fill in the rest of the zodiac around the circle in sequence, one across each sector boundary. If you've forgotten the sequence, look at the diagram on page 16. When you've done that, draw a symbol for the Sun (☉—a circle with a point at its centre) in one of the sectors which has your Sun sign at its edge. Think about how far through the sign your Sun is; make sure that you have put it in the right sector. Whichever sector this is will be very important to you; having the Sun there gives a bias to the whole chart, like the weight on one side of a locomotive wheel. You will feel that the activities of that sector (or house, as they are usually called) are most in keeping with your character, and you feel comfortable doing that sort of thing.

Make sure you have got your sums right. As a Sagittarius born in the afternoon, you might well have Taurus rising, and the Sun in the eighth house, for example.

Now is the time to examine the twelve numbered sections of your own sky, and see what there is to be found.

Angular Houses: 1, 4, 7, 10

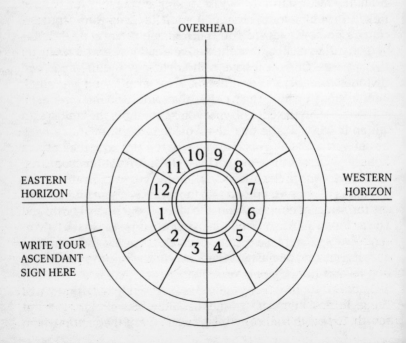

These are the houses closest to the horizon and the vertical, reading round in zodiacal sequence. The first house is concerned with you yourself as a physical entity, your appearance, and your health. Most of this has been dealt with in the section on Ascendants. If you have the Sun here, it simply doubles the impact of your Sun sign energies.

Opposite to you is the seventh house, which concerns itself with everybody who is not you. Partners in a business sense, husbands, wives, enemies you are actually aware of (and who therefore stand opposed to you in plain sight) and any other unclassified strangers all belong in the seventh house. You see their motivation as being of the opposite sign to your Ascendant sign, as being something you are not. If you have Capricorn rising, you see them as behaving, and needing to be treated, which is perhaps more accurate, in a Cancerian manner. This is how you approach seventh-house things. Use the keywords from 'The Meaning of the Zodiac' (p. 17) to remind yourself what this is. If you have the Sun in the seventh house you are your own best partner: you may marry late in life, or not at all. Perhaps your marriage will be unsuccessful. It is not a failure; it is simply that you are to a very great extent self-supporting, and have neither the ability nor the need to share yourself completely with another.

The whole business of the first and the seventh is to do with 'me and not-me'. For the personal energies of this relationship to be shown in tangible form, it is necessary to look at the pair of houses whose axis most squarely crosses the first/seventh axis. This is the fourth/tenth. The tenth is your received status in the world, and is the actual answer to the question 'What do you take me for?' No matter what you do, the world will find it best to see you as doing the sort of thing shown by the sign at the start of the tenth house. Eventually, you will start to pursue that kind of activity anyway, because in doing so you get more appreciation and reward from the rest of society.

Your efforts in dealing with others, which is a first/seventh thing, have their result in the tenth, and their origins in the fourth. Expect to find clues there to your family, your home, the beliefs you hold most dear, and the eventual conclusion to your life (not your death, which is a different matter). If you have the Sun in the tenth, you will achieve some measure of prominence or fame; if your Sun is in the fourth, you will do well in property, and your family will be of greater importance to you than is usual.

There is, of course, some give and take between the paired houses. Giving more time to yourself in the first house means that you are denying attention to the seventh, your partner; the reverse also applies. Giving a lot of attention to your career, in the tenth house, stops you from spending quite so much time as you might like with your family or at home. Spending too much time at home means that you are out of the public eye. There is only so much time in a day; what you give to one must be denied to the other.

This cross of four houses defines most people's lives: self, partner, home, and career. An over-emphasis on any of these is to the detriment of the other three, and all the arms of the cross feel and react to any event affecting any single member.

If these four houses have cardinal signs on them in your chart, then you are very much the sort of person who feels that he is in control of his own life, and that it is his duty to shape it into something new, personal, and original. You feel that by making decisive moves with your own circumstances you can actually change the way your life unfolds, and enjoy steering it the way you want it to go.

If these four houses have fixed signs on them in your chart, then you are the sort of person who sees the essential shape of your life as being one of looking after what you were given, continuing in the tradition, and ending up with a profit at the end of it all. Like a farmer, you see yourself as a tenant of the land you inherited, with a responsibility to hand it on in at least as good a condition as it was when you took it over. You are likely to see the main goal in all life's ups and downs as the maintenance of stability and enrichment of what you possess.

If these four houses have mutable signs on them in your chart, then you are much more willing to change yourself to suit circumstances than the other two. Rather than seeing yourself as the captain of your ship, or the trustee of the family firm, you see yourself as free to adapt to challenges as they arise, and if necessary to make fundamental changes in your life, home and career to suit the needs of the moment. You are the sort to welcome change and novelty, and you don't expect to have anything to show for it at the end of the day except experience. There is a strong sense of service in the mutable signs, and if you spend your life working for the welfare of others, then they will have something to show for it while you will not. Not in physical terms, anyway; you will have had your reward by seeing your own energies transformed into their success.

The Succedent Houses: 2, 5, 8, 11

These houses are called succedent because they succeed, or follow on from, the previous four. Where the angular houses define the framework of the life, the succedent ones give substance, and help develop it to its fullest and richest extent, in exactly the same way as fixed signs show the development and maintenance of the elemental energies defined by the cardinal signs.

The second house and the eighth define your resources; how much you have to play with, so to speak. The fifth and eleventh show what you do with it, and how much you achieve. Your immediate environment is the business of the second house. Your tastes in furniture and clothes are here (all part of your immediate environment, if you think about it) as well as your immediate resources, food and cash. Food is a resource because without it you are short of energy, and cash is a resource for obvious reasons. If you have the Sun here you are likely to be fond of spending money, and fond of eating too! You are likely to place value on things that you can buy or possess, and judge your success by your bank balance.

Opposed to it, and therefore dealing with the opposite viewpoint, is the eighth house, where you will find stored money. Savings, bank accounts, mortgages, and all kinds of non-immediate money come under this house. So do major and irreversible changes in your life, because they are the larger environment rather than the immediate one. Surgical operations and death are both in the eighth, because you are not the same person afterwards, and that is an irreversible change. If you have the Sun in the eighth you are likely to be very careful with yourself, and not the sort to expose yourself to any risk; you are also not likely to be short of a few thousand when life gets tight, because eighth house people always have some extra resource tucked away somewhere. You are also likely to benefit from legacies, which are another form of long-term wealth.

To turn all this money into some form of visible wealth you must obviously do something with it, and all forms of self-expression and ambition are found in the fifth and the eleventh houses. The fifth is where you have fun, basically; all that you like to do, all that amuses you, all your hobbies are found there, and a look at the zodiac sign falling in that house in your chart will show you what it is that you like so much. Your children are a fifth-house phenomenon, too; they are an expression of yourself made physical, made from the substance of your body and existence, and given their own. If you have the Sun in the fifth house you are likely to be of a generally happy disposition, confident that life is there to be enjoyed, and sure that something good will turn up.

The eleventh house, in contrast, is not so much what you like doing as what you would like to be doing: it deals with hopes, wishes, and ambitions. It also deals with friends and all social gatherings, because in a similar manner to the Aries/Libra axis, anybody who is 'not-you' and enjoying themselves must be opposed to you enjoying yourself in the fifth house. If you have the Sun in the eleventh house, you are at your best in a group. You would do well in large organizations, possibly political ones, and will find that you can organize well. You have well-defined ambitions, and know how to realize them, using other people as supporters of your cause.

The oppositions in this cross work just as effectively as the previous set did: cash is either used or stored, and to convert it from one to the other diminishes the first. Similarly, time spent enjoying yourself does nothing for your ambitions and aims, nor does it help you maintain relationships with all the groups of people you know; there again, all work and no play . . .

If you have cardinal signs on these four houses in your chart, then you think that using all the resources available to you at any one time is important. Although what you do isn't necessarily important, or even stable, you want to have something to show for it, and enjoying yourself as you go along is important to you. To you, money is for spending, and how your friends see you is possibly more important to you than how you see yourself.

Fixed signs on these four houses will make you reticent, and careful of how you express yourself. You are possibly too busy with the important things of life as you see them, such as your career and long-term prospects, to give much attention to the way you live. You feel it is important to have things of quality, because you have a long-term view of life, and you feel secure when you have some money in the bank, but you don't enjoy your possessions and friends for your own sake. You have them because you feel that you should, not because they are reason enough in themselves.

Mutable signs on these four houses show a flexible attitude to the use of a resource, possibly because the angular houses show that you already have plenty of it, and it is your duty to use it well. You don't mind spending time and money on projects which to you are necessary, and which will have a measurable end result. You see that you need to spend time and effort to bring projects into a completed reality, and you are willing to do that as long as the final product is yours and worth having. You are likely to change your style of living quite frequently during your life, and there may be ambitions which, when fulfilled, fade from your life completely.

The Cadent Houses: 3, 6, 9, 12

The final four houses are called cadent either because they fall away from the angles (horizon and vertical axes), or because they

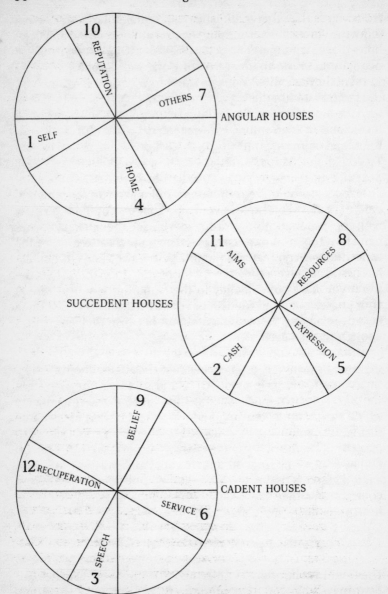

ANGULAR HOUSES

10 REPUTATION
1 SELF
OTHERS 7
HOME 4

SUCCEDENT HOUSES

11 AIMS
8 RESOURCES
2 CASH
EXPRESSION 5

CADENT HOUSES

9 BELIEF
12 RECUPERATION
SPEECH 3
SERVICE 6

fall towards them, giving their energy towards the formation of the next phase in their existence. Either way, affairs in these houses are nothing like as firm and active as those in the other two sets of four. It may be useful to think of them as being given to mental rather than physical or material activities.

The third and ninth houses are given to thought and speech, with the ninth specializing in incoming thoughts, such as reading, learning and belief (religions of all kinds are ninth-house things), while the third limits itself to speaking and writing, daily chat, and the sort of conversations you have every day. If you have the Sun in the third house, you will be a chatterbox. Talking is something you could do all day, and you love reading. Anything will do—papers, magazines, novels; as long as it has words in it you will like it. You will have the sort of mind that loves accumulating trivia, but you may find that serious study or hard learning is something that you cannot do.

The third house concerns itself with daily conversation, but the ninth is more withdrawn. Study is easy for a ninth-house person, but since all ideal and theoretical thought belongs here, the down-to-earth street-corner reality of the third house doesn't, and so the higher knowledge of the ninth finds no application in daily life. The third-ninth axis is the difference between practical street experience and the refined learning of a university. To give time to one must mean taking time from the other. If you have the Sun in the ninth, you are likely to have a very sure grasp of the theory of things, and could well be an instigator or director of large projects; but you are unable to actually do the things yourself. Knowledge is yours, but application is not.

How this knowledge gets applied in the production of something new is a matter of technique, and technique is the business of the sixth house. The way things get done, both for yourself and for other people's benefit, is all in the sixth. Everything you do on someone else's behalf is there, too. If you have the Sun in the sixth house, you are careful and considerate by nature, much concerned to make the best use of things and to do things in the best way possible. Pride of work and craftsmanship are guiding words to you; any kind of sloppiness is upsetting. You look after yourself, too; health is a sixth-house thing, and the Sun in the sixth sometimes makes you something of a hypochondriac.

Opposed to the sixth, and therefore opposed to the ideas of doing things for others, mastering the proper technique, and looking after your physical health, is the twelfth house. This is concerned with withdrawing yourself from the world, being on your own, having time to think. Energy is applied to the job in hand in the sixth house, and here it is allowed to grow again without being applied to anything. Recuperation is a good word to remember. All forms of rest are twelfth-house concepts. If you have the Sun in the twelfth house you are an essentially private individual, and there will be times when you need to be on your own to think about things and recover your strength and balance. You will keep your opinions to yourself, and share very little of your emotional troubles with anyone. Yours is most definitely not a life lived out in the open.

These houses live in the shadow of the houses which follow them. Each of them is a preparation for the next phase. If your Sun is in any of these houses, your life is much more one of giving away than of accumulation. You already have the experience and the knowledge, and you will be trying to hand it on before you go, so to speak. Acquisition is something you will never manage on a permanent basis.

If these houses have Cardinal signs on them in your chart, then preparation for things to come is important to you, and you think in straight lines towards a recognized goal. You will have firm and rather simplistic views and beliefs about matters which are not usually described in such terms, such as morality and politics, and you will be used to saying things simply and with meaning. Deception and half-truths, even mild exaggeration, confuse you, because you do not think in that sort of way.

If fixed signs occupy these houses in your horoscope, your thinking is conservative, and your mind, though rich and varied in its imagination, is not truly original. You like to collect ideas from elsewhere and tell yourself that they are your own. You rely on changing circumstances to bring you variety, and your own beliefs and opinions stay fixed to anchor you in a changing world; unfortunately, this can mean a refusal to take in new ideas, shown in your behaviour as a rather appealing old-fashionedness.

Having mutable signs on these houses in your horoscope shows a flexible imagination, though often not a very practical one. Speech and ideas flow freely from you, and you are quick to adapt your ideas to suit the occasion, performing complete changes of viewpoint without effort if required. You seem to have grasped the instinctive truth that mental images and words are not real, and can be changed or erased at will; you are far less inhibited in their use than the other two groups, who regard words as something at least as heavy as cement, and nearly as difficult to dissolve. Periods in the public eye and periods of isolation are of equal value to you; you can use them each for their best purpose, and have no dislike of either. This great flexibility of mind does mean, though, that you lack seriousness of approach at times, and have a happy-go-lucky view of the future, and of things spiritual, which may lead to eventual disappointments and regrets.

Houses are important in a horoscope. The twelve sectors of the sky correspond to the twelve signs of the zodiac, the difference being that the zodiac is a product of the Sun's annual revolution, and the houses are a product (via the Ascendant) of the Earth's daily revolution. They bring the symbolism down one level from the sky to the individual, and they answer the questions which arise when people of the same Sun sign have different lives and different preferences. The house in which the Sun falls, and the qualities of the signs in the houses, show each person's approach to those areas of his life, and the one which will be the most important to him.

Part 4

Sagittarius Trivia

7. Tastes and Preferences

Clothes

Sagittarian taste in clothes is virtually non-existent—they are often the scruffiest people in the whole zodiac. The reason isn't hard to fathom—it is all to do with the need for movement, and the dislike of anything formal or restricting, that characterizes everything else about the sign.

It's not that the Sagittarian intends to be under-dressed for the occasion; it's just that none of the reasons for dressing up have any meaning for him. For example, people often dress smartly when they are in a formal situation, such as going to a wedding, or to a job interview. This is done to show a form of respect to the social position of the other person present, or in the hope that they might think well of you. Sagittarius is interested in neither of these ideas: he only shows respect when he thinks people merit it (and sees no reason why he should do it among friends at a wedding), and he is confident enough in himself not to care whether people think well of him or not. If they don't, that's their loss. Some people also dress up to make themselves feel better—but Sagittarius feels fine anyway, because he always has Jupiter to cheer him up. Finally, many formal clothes, being Saturnine in nature and purpose, are physically restricting—ties and suits for men, suits and court shoes for women—which Sagittarians see as an uncomfortable restriction on their movements, and so to be avoided if at all possible.

Whatever they wear, Sagittarians are fond of blue. It is used to show how relaxed they are about things, and how easy of access, unlike the intense and slightly hostile effect of the bright red favoured by Arians and some Scorpios. Apart from this preference for blue, Sagittarians have no other particular favourite colours, but will wear anything which strikes them as likeable and fun.

There is an element of the outdoors in Sagittarian clothes. Even in the most restricted situation, they will find a way of putting in some reference to travelling, foreign lands, or horses. Their clothes are always chosen with outdoor use in mind; where another sign might look at a jacket and ask himself whether it was in this year's style, a Sagittarian looks at it and wonders how it will stand up to pouring rain, and how useful the pockets are.

Jeans are the great Sagittarian garment. They are informal, they are tough, they have an image associated with travel and adventure, they emphasize the thighs, the Sagittarian part of the body, and they are blue.

Sagittarian style, if there is such a thing, takes clothes from anything associated with travelling or horses. Riding boots, hacking jackets, cravats; jumpsuits and flying jackets from the pioneer aviator days; leather jackets from motorcycling; jeans from the American West; big sweaters and anoraks from mountaineers and polar explorers. In addition, anything that is recognizably from distant lands, such as India or China, finds a home in the Sagittarian wardrobe.

Food and Furnishings

Sagittarian taste in food is simple—you like everything. Endlessly energetic, and so perpetually hungry, you will eat whatever is put in front of you. With this sign, the countries or lifestyles associated with the food are as interesting as the food itself: hence a love of fast food, because of its association with the open spaces and the automobile-based culture of the United States. You love Indian food too, because of its associations with distant places. Lastly, Sagittarians are fond of all sorts of game; perhaps the connection is with the Archer who is the top half of the sign. Anything that is usually shot before it is eaten, from hare to venison, you will find to your taste.

A Sagittarian house is a glorious cross between a junk shop, a sports shop, and a library. Wherever you go, there are books, usually supplemented by piles of magazines on every possible subject. There are also various 'interesting things', which Sagittarians acquire on their travels, and never throw away.

Sagittarian rooms are seldom blue, despite the preferences of the sign: warm reds and browns are much more common, because, more than anything else, a Sagittarian home is warm and welcoming, for friends and visitors as well as the owner. Furniture is comfortable first, stylish later in these places; the essential idea is to provide somewhere for people to sit, talk, read, and play. In a Sagittarian house, maps and magazines are laid out on the floor as travel plans are discussed; there is a smell of coffee and toast as Sagittarian appetites are catered for in an informal way; and large dogs, Sagittarian favourites, wander in and out begging titbits from visitors in an appealing fashion.

Hobbies

To say that Sagittarians enjoy travelling in their spare time is to misunderstand the essence of the sign. Sagittarians travel as a way of life: they have jobs in their spare time, from nine to five, Monday to Friday.

The actual process of travelling is in itself exciting and rewarding for a Sagittarian. Stevenson, the man who said that 'to travel hopefully is a better thing than to arrive', was a Sagittarian. He also said, 'I travel for travel's sake. The great affair is to move', and wrote Treasure Island, of course—a Sagittarian story if ever there was one.

Methods of transport are often interesting in themselves to Sagittarians; many are devoted to open-top sports cars, old biplanes, or motorcycles. In each case, the attraction is the sensation of speed, the exhilaration of feeling yourself travel.

Naturally all forms of equestrian sport appeal, but so do all team games: Sagittarians are better team athletes than individual performers, because they like the friendly feeling of the team spirit.

On the rare days when he isn't active, the Sagittarian will sit and read, so that his mind does the exploring instead. He will read almost anything: history, biography, the lot. A Sagittarian likes novels which are full of action, and will seldom read romantic fiction, but apart from that absolutely anything goes.

8. Sagittarian Luck

Being lucky isn't a matter of pure luck. It can be engineered. What happens when you are lucky is that a number of correspondences are made between circumstances, people, and even material items, which eventually enable planetary energies to flow quickly and effectively to act with full force in a particular way. If you are part of that chain, or your intentions lie in the same direction as the planetary flow, then you say that things are going your way, or that you are lucky. All you have to do to maximize this tendency is to make sure you are aligned to the flow of energies from the planets whenever you want things to work your way.

It is regular astrological practice to try to reinforce your own position in these things, by attracting energies which are already strongly represented in you. For a Sagittarius, this means Jupiter, of course, and therefore any 'lucky' number, colour, or whatever for a Sagittarius is simply going to be one which corresponds symbolically to the attributes of Jupiter.

Jupiter's colour is blue; therefore a Sagittarian's lucky colour is blue, because by wearing it or aligning himself to it, for example by betting on a horse whose jockey's silks are blue, or supporting a sporting team whose colours include blue, he aligns himself to the energies of Jupiter, and thereby recharges the solar energies that are already in him.

A Sagittarius's preferred gemstone is amethyst; topaz is often quoted too. Gemstones are seen as being able to concentrate or focus magical energies, and the colour of the stone shows its propensity to the energies of a particular planet. There are other stones quoted for the sign, such as sapphire and zircon, but in most cases it is the colour which is the key.

Because Sagittarius is the ninth sign, your lucky number is 9; all combinations of numbers which add up to 9 by reduction work the same way, so you have a range to choose from. Reducing a number is done by adding its digits until you can go no further. As an example, take 486; $4 + 8 + 6 = 18$, and then $1 + 8 = 9$. There you are—486 is a lucky number for you, so to buy a car with those digits in its registration plate would make it a car which, while you had it, you were very fond of, and which served you well.

Jupiter has its own number, which is 3 (though some authorities quote 4). The same rules apply as they did with 9. Jupiter also has its own day, Thursday (jeudi in French, which is Jupiter's day, yes?), and Sagittarius has a direction with which it is associated, the East. If you have something important to do, and you manage to put it into action on Thursday 3rd September (month number 9, remember), then you will have made sure that you will get the result best suited to you, by aligning yourself to your own planet and helping its energies flow through you and your activity unimpeded.

Jupiter also has a metal associated with it, and in the Middle Ages people wore jewellery made of their planetary metals for luck, or self-alignment and emphasis, whichever way you want to describe it. In the case of Sagittarius and Jupiter, that metal is tin. Tin jewellery doesn't sound very attractive, I know, but nowadays the alloy known as pewter is almost pure tin, and there are all sorts of pewter ornaments about; beer tankards spring to mind as an example, which is the sort of sociable and cheerful thing a Sagittarian would make from his metal!

There are plants and herbs for each planet, and foods too. Among Jupiter's plants are cloves and nutmeg, the herbs marjoram and borage, fruits like strawberries, gooseberries and raisins—and rhubarb! There is almost no end to the list of correspondences between the planets and everyday items, and many more can be made if you have a good imagination. They are lucky for Sagittarius if you know what makes them so, and if you believe them to be so; the essence of the process lies in linking yourself and the object of your intent with some identifiable token of your own planet, such as its colour or number, and strengthening yourself thereby. The stronger you are, then the more frequently you will be able to achieve the result you want—and that's all that luck is, isn't it?

A Final Word

By the time you reach here, you will have learnt a great deal more about yourself. At least, I hope you have.

You will probably have noticed that I appear to have contradicted myself in some parts of the book, and repeated myself in others, and there are reasons for this. It is quite likely that I have said that your Sun position makes you one way, while your Ascendant makes you the opposite. There is nothing strange about this; nobody is consistent, the same the whole way through—everybody has contradictory sides to their character, and knowing some more about your Sun sign and your Ascendant will help you to label and define those contradictory elements. It won't do anything about dealing with them, though—that's your job, and always has been. The only person who can live your horoscope is you. Astrology won't make your problems disappear, and it never has been able to; it simply defines the problems more clearly, and enables you to look for answers.

Where I have repeated myself it is either to make the point for the benefit of the person who is only going to read that section of the book, or because you have a double helping of the energy of your sign, as in the instance of the Sun and Ascendant in the same sign.

I hope you found the relationships section useful; you may well find that the Sun-to-Ascendant comparison is just as useful in showing you how you fit in with your partner as the usual Sun-to-Sun practice.

Where do you go from here? If you want to learn more about astrology, and see how all of the planets fit into the picture of the sky as it was at your birth, then you must either consult an astrologer or learn how to do it for yourself. There is quite a lot of astrology around these days; evening classes are not too hard to find and there are groups of enthusiasts up and down the country. There are also plenty of books which will show you how to draw up and interpret your own horoscope.

One thing about doing it yourself, which is an annoyance unless you are aware of it in advance: to calculate your horoscope properly you will need to know where the planets were in the sky when you were born, and you usually have to buy this data separately in a book called an ephemeris. The reason that astrology books don't have this data in them is that to include enough for everybody who is likely to buy the book would make the book as big as a phone directory, and look like a giant book of log tables, which is a bit off-putting. You can buy ephemerides (the plural) for any single year, such as the one of your birth. You can also buy omnibus versions for the whole century.

So, you will need two books, not one: an ephemeris, and a book to help you draw up and interpret your horoscope. It's much less annoying when you *know* you're going to need two books.

After that, there are lots of books on the more advanced techniques in the Astrology Handbook series, also from the Aquarian Press. Good though the books are, there is no substitute for being taught by an astrologer, and no substitute at all for practice. What we are trying to do here is provide a vocabulary of symbols taken from the sky so that you and your imagination can make sense of the world you live in; the essential element is your imagination, and you provide that.

Astrology works perfectly well at Sun sign level, and it works perfectly well at deeper levels as well; you can do it with what you want. I hope that, whatever you do with it, it is both instructive and satisfying to you—and fun, too.

SUNS AND LOVERS

The Astrology of Sexual Relationships

Penny Thornton. It doesn't seem to matter how experienced –
or inexperienced – you are, when it comes to love and romance
there just *isn't* a fool proof formula. . . but this book does its best
to provide one! THE definitive astrological guide to sexual
relationships, this book is based upon the accumulated wisdom,
and observations of centuries of dedicated astrologers. Reveals:

- In-depth analysis of astrological types
- Male and female profiles for each star sign
- Zodiacal attitudes to intimate relationships
- Most compatible – and incompatible – partners

Each general star sign analysis is concluded with amazingly
frank reflections, often based upon personal interviews, with
many famous personalities including: Bob Champion; Suzi
Quatro; Colin Wilson; Jeremy Irons; HRH The Princess Anne;
HRH The Duke of York; Martin Shaw; Barbara Cartland; Twiggy
and many more. Written in an easy-to-read style, and packed
with illuminating and fascinating tit-bits, this book is compulsive
reading for anyone likely to have *any sort* of encounter with the
opposite sex!